THE 28-DAY
THOUGHT
DIET

Compiled by Vanessa Lowry · Edited by Nanette Littlestone

Christian Belz · Sandy Weaver Carman · Kristin Colier · Martha Forlines
Betty Humphrey Fowler · David Greer · Kelly Greer · Andy Greider
Patricia Hayes · Jim Hogan · Dr. Robin Kirby · Ginnie Faye Liman
Nanette Littlestone · Traci Long · Vanessa Lowry · Cheryl Anne McGill
Laura McGill · Tricia Molloy · Jennifer Moore · Monserrat del Carmen Pineda
Kathryn Sener · Sharon S. Smith · Mindy Strich · Jeanie Ward · Kyle Young

Cover Art & Layout Design by: **Vanessa Lowry, www.connect4leverage.com**

Editing by: **Nanette Littlestone, www.wordsofpassion.com**

Printing by: **BookLogix Publishing Services, Inc., www.booklogix.com**

First Edition Printed, 2013

This book may be purchased in bulk for educational, business, fundraising, or
sales promotional use. For information please contact:
Vanessa Lowry, www.connect4leverage.com

This book is designed to provide accurate information in regard to the subject
matter covered. It is sold with the understanding that the publisher is not
engaged in rendering legal, accounting, or other professional services. If you
require legal advice or other expert assistance, you should seek the services
of a competent professional.

ISBN: 978-0-615-75388-1

Printed in the United States of America

Dedicated to you, the person willing to choose a better thought upon which to focus, making a positive change in your own life and in the world.

Contents

Contents

No matter what is happening in our lives, we choose how we wish to think about it. And the greatest gift we give ourselves is often our willingness to change our minds.

~ Marianne Williamson

Introduction

by Vanessa Lowry

What were you just thinking? Were you feeling rushed? Anxious? Irritated? Curious? Peaceful? The number of thoughts a person has each day range from 12,000 to 70,000. For the majority of people, up to 80% of these thoughts are negative.

Thought leaders believe we change our lives by choosing our thoughts. In his book *Wishes Fulfilled,* Dr. Wayne Dyer encourages you, the reader, to visualize a conveyor belt running through your head filled with a continuous stream of thoughts. At any time, you can choose to place the thought you are currently holding back onto the conveyor belt and pick up a different thought.

The authors of this book share their personal experience around a specific topic each day. Our goal is to encourage you to observe your thoughts and inspire you to choose a thought that grows your life in a more fulfilling and joyful way.

For the next 28 days, change your life by choosing to hold thoughts that energize and support you. You'll always have a combination of thoughts that assist you in living a life you love along with those that don't serve you as well. Making a commitment to be aware of your thoughts and consciously choosing a better thought for 28 days will allow you to measure how this new practice affects your life and the way it alters how others interact with you.

When we are no longer able to change a situation, we are challenged to change ourselves. ~ Victor Frankl

Day 1

Today, I choose a thought of

Gratitude Adjustment

by Mindy Strich

Gratitude unlocks the fullness of life. It turns what we have into enough, and more. It turns denial into acceptance, chaos into order, and confusion into clarity. It turns problems into gifts, failures into success, the unexpected into perfect timing, and mistakes into important events. Gratitude makes sense of our past, brings peace for today, and creates a vision for tomorrow.
~ Melodie Beattie

Every morning the alarm on my iPhone goes off and reminds me to "Awake with Gratitude." It sets my day in motion.

A large percentage of the thoughts we have consist more of what we don't have instead of what we do. We don't have enough time, we don't have enough money, "Mr. Right" turned out to be "Mr. Wrong."

I empathize. It's hard to see the blessings while we are in the midst of life's challenges. And that's exactly when we need gratitude most.

Two years ago I experienced an unexpected separation from my husband. I was profoundly sad, extremely scared, and completely overwhelmed. I didn't set any alarm in the morning because most days I could barely get out of bed. Gratitude was the last thing on my mind and certainly nowhere in my heart.

One by one things in my house started breaking down. First, the air conditioning system stopped working in the middle of a heat wave. A water pipe broke and flooded the bathroom and the basement. The final blow occurred during a thunder storm when a tree hit my house, destroying the back deck and the roof. It was truly a miracle I wasn't killed. Three feet closer and I might have been.

In more ways than one, thankfully, the crash woke me up while I was asleep.

What we resist persists. What we focus on expands. If it's true that human beings have up to 60,000 thoughts a day, 59,000 of mine consisted of my life falling apart and that I was losing everything. It shouldn't have come as a big surprise to me that my house began to fall apart, and if not for a near miss of an oak tree, I would have lost everything.

I could no longer ignore the signs. I needed a "gratitude" adjustment.

I set my intention to find the gifts. When the voices in my head relentlessly repeated what I didn't have and never would (no job, no money, no one to love and take care of me) I asked my heart to guide me in the direction of gratitude.

I started focusing my attention on appreciating everyone and everything. I was grateful for every meal and everyone that contributed to my sustenance. I gave thanks to the earth and the sun, the wind and the rain, the birds and the bees. To my arms and my legs, my heart and my lungs, all 50 trillion cells that filled my senses and gave me life. My iPhone and flat iron, toothbrush, and hairbrush, even the customer service rep at Comcast who had me on hold for twenty minutes all got props. I saw unconditional love in the eyes of my dog Karma and found a beautiful poem that summed it up.

Even after all this time the sun never says to the earth 'You Owe Me' and look what happens with a love like that. It lights up the whole sky. ~ Hafiz, *The Sun Never Says*

As I began to practice gratitude I also saw how much I was taking for granted.

In the places where gratitude seemed impossible to find I was determined to search for the gifts. When the grief became too much to bear I repeated over and over "What are the gifts? Where are the gifts?" And one day at a time, one thought at a time, the answers started to slowly appear.

- What are the gifts in feeling alone and unloved?
  Learning how to be independent and love yourself.

- Where are the gifts in not having money?
  Appreciating what you do have that doesn't cost money. Finding trust and having faith that you will always have what you need.

My broken heart opened me up to discover that gratitude was the treasure that transformed me.

Giving birth is physically one of the most painful events a woman's body can withstand, yet we endure the pain to get the prize—the creation of a new life.

Laboring through my pain, allowed me to use gratitude to see new life. I became more accepting, more understanding, and more compassionate.

Feeling lost was empowering me to find myself, to discover new people, new places, and new experiences I never could have imagined.

Being lonely pushed me to venture out and make new friends, face my fears, and take some risks. Becoming self-reliant enabled me to learn to take care of myself.

The emotional and physical despair I felt led me to renewal and recovery through a course on energetic healing and the greatest gift of all—my unforeseen career as an Energetic Healer.

Last Thanksgiving I listened affectionately to everyone express what they were most grateful for: their children, their parents, their health, their spouse. When it was my turn I felt tears in my eyes when I spoke from my heart. "Sometimes when I think about all the things I am grateful for it takes my breath away. I am profoundly thankful for all of it, but I think I am especially thankful for all that appears on the surface to suggest no visible offers of gratitude. When we dig deeper, those are the things in which, perhaps, we should be most grateful."

Mindy Strich is a certified I.E.M. Energetic Healer and owner of Healing Hearts, LLC. Locating energetic imbalances, Mindy assists clients that are experiencing physical or emotional pain to activate the body's natural ability to heal. **www.healingheartenergy.com**

Today, I choose a thought of
Joyful Waiting

by Kelly Greer

I hate to wait. Does anyone like to wait? Does it ever seem like that's all you do? If you have kids this is especially true. Lots of waiting.

Before I go any further, I must make a confession… I am a certified Type A (with a capital A), often over-the-top, Control Freak. I'm trying to do better. Really. Today I call myself a "recovering" control freak, but I still fall into full-blown nepotism from time to time. Control Freaks, in particular, do not like to wait because it amplifies the fact that they are not in control. My disdain of waiting varies from the small—"I can't believe it is taking 30 seconds to reheat my coffee"—to the large—"Why haven't all my dreams and goals happened yet?"

However, I made a discovery recently that has totally changed my outlook on waiting. Before this discovery I could see absolutely no value in waiting and viewed my periods of waiting—both large and small—as voids of time forever lost with no redeeming qualities. This has been especially true as I reflect on where I am today and where I want to go. So be impatient about the coffee maker and microwave if you must, but I want to encourage you to look differently at the art of waiting as it relates to your station and calling in life.

First of all, the fact that you feel like you have a calling or purpose or dream implies some type of promise from *somewhere*. As a believer, I believe that this is from God. I believe that as I give my life to Christ, He begins to impart His dreams and goals and plans for my life into my heart. I believe that there is a good and perfect plan for my life. The question becomes am I going to follow my own plans or trust that God has the better one for me?

Several years ago God spoke into my heart very clearly something He wanted me to do. I met His idea with both excitement and a certain amount of disbelief. I was excited because I saw real value and purpose in what He was asking me to do. I was also excited because this was the first time I had received an assignment that I was certain was from Him. The disbelief came because I was pretty sure He had the wrong girl. While I possessed some of the skill sets required for this task, I felt so very ill equipped for much of it. And so the journey began. There's nothing quite like being on step 1, seeing step 10, and having no real clue on how you are going to get from here to there. I have learned so much since that time almost 5 years ago—spiritual lessons on faith, truth, hope, doubt, prayer, and fears. I've learned very tangible lessons too—growth in the areas of writing, speaking, social media, culture, empathy, and more. But perhaps one of the biggest lessons I'm learning is what to do with the reality of waiting.

I love how author and priest *Henri Nouwen* views waiting:

People who wait have received a promise that allows them to wait. They have received something that is at work in them, like a seed that has started to grow. This is very important. We can only really wait if what we are waiting for has already begun for us. So waiting is never a movement from nothing to something. It is always a movement from something to something more.

I don't think I would have ever chosen it for myself, but I've become a student of waiting. I've learned about "active waiting," which is the idea of being *fully present* in the moment. It's believing that something is always happening right where you are, even if it doesn't look like it. And you know what? It's true!

I've learned to wait without "overthinking it." So often I think that if I just think about something MORE, I'll figure it out. Sometimes that's true, but most of the time, at least for me, all it serves to do is make me mean, exhausted, and give me a headache! Sometimes "rational thinking" is the enemy of revelation from God. We weren't meant to "figure everything out." What is asked of us is to seek, trust, and obey God. When He asks us to do something, do it. Wait. Repeat. I'm not talking about being a drone and turning off your brain, but I am talking about realizing that it is possible to overthink something to the point of just making yourself nuts!

I've learned that waiting is a requirement for the spiritual life and doing what God put each of us on earth to do. But when we wait with Jesus it's never wasted time, and, most importantly, when we wait with Him we can wait with hope and assurance. When God makes you a promise He doesn't change His mind. It may not happen how you think it should or in the time frame you think it will, but it will happen if you don't give up on it.

> For the vision is yet for an appointed time, but at the end it shall speak, and not lie: though it tarries, wait for it; because it will surely come, it will not delay. ~ Habakkuk 2:3

So I wait.

Sometimes I think I'm waiting on God. Much of the time I think God is waiting on me and my fat head. Most of the time I have no clue what's the holdup and the reality is, it doesn't matter! But one thing I know; I will come to vision. Do you believe that for yourself and your God-given dreams? I absolutely do.

I wait expectantly.

I wait patiently.

I wait with and for the Holy Spirit to do His work in me.

I wait with joy!

Kelly Greer is a summa cum laude graduate of the "Been there, ought not to have done that" School of Bad Decisions. Kelly brings a realness, compassion, and a deeply personal understanding of God's amazing grace and help that is available for all who seek it. A gifted encourager and self-described "show me the steps" analytic, Kelly offers step-by-step help to living a life of peace, purpose, love, and happiness regardless of current circumstances or an "exciting" past. **www.gwinnettmagazine.com**

Today, I choose a thought of

Small Steps

by Kyle Young

BIGGER is better! We hear the message everywhere. It seems the focus is always on the big success, the grand gesture, the mega business deal. And so we fall into the trap of thinking that one small "something" won't make a difference. Why bother to vote? Just one vote won't really count. How will skipping that one cupcake matter when you need to lose 25 pounds? What's the use of sending a simple "thank you" note, when you really need to write a BIG contract?

Well, take a lesson from Mother Nature. Have you ever been stung by a bee? OUCH! That one small insect can ruin your entire day. And you thought small things didn't matter. Yes, in a world that's constantly pushing us to do more, have more, be more . . . it is easy to forget the amazing power of small.

We're told to set big goals, make big plans, have big dreams, and just overall think BIG. And that's a good thing . . . unless, of course, you're so overwhelmed by the big that it keeps you from taking the first small step! Or, even worse, if you fall short of your goal, you just throw up your hands and give up entirely. Well, don't! It's time to embrace the small things—the things you can do right now, the simple steps you can take—and watch as they add up to make a big difference.

You may be surprised when you take the opportunity to reflect, refocus, and reconsider small. I had a great chance to do this myself recently. My husband and I, at the urging of our teenage son, rejoined the gym we'd given up years before when he was born. For a while, we did a pretty good job of working out there 3 or 4 times a week. But then life happened. My husband had some serious health issues and the gym trips were one of the first things to fall off our schedule.

But that was last year. When he, thankfully, returned to full health, what was my excuse? Hmmmm. I spent a lot of time and mental energy knowing I should be exercising and, of course, coming up with all kinds of reasons why I just didn't "have the time." Then one morning, my inbox included a note from a fitness coach friend. She was hosting a "10 Minute Trainer" virtual workout group. Ten minutes? Okay, that got my attention. Even I could find 10 minutes a day, I thought. It was a "no brainer," so I signed on.

Taking that simple step of claiming a tiny ten minutes of time for workouts I could do at home—on my own schedule—began making a difference. I, who have never been very athletic and pretty much "hated" to exercise, found myself working out not just ten, but some days twenty, or thirty minutes! Even on days I was "too tired," or was legitimately pressed for time, I COULD STILL DO 10 MINUTES. I had found one small thing that I could stick with, and I began seeing results!

Here's another quick example. Attending a writer's workshop recently, I heard an award-winning author praise the "discipline" of sitting down and writing just one page a day. . . every day. "If you do that, you'll write about 300 words. By the end of a year, you will have written the average-length novel." Think about it! How many of us have said, "Someday I'll write a book," but our brilliant idea just never seems to become reality. What would happen if you took that "someday" and committed to a simple and doable writing one page a day? There you'd have it!

Your challenge could even be something as simple as finding a bit of "down time." When we're over-worked and over-stressed, we may dream of an *Eat. Pray. Love.* leave-it-all-behind getaway. But really, how many of us can manage that? So what CAN we do? Take a 5-minute vacation. "What I need is 5 weeks!" I hear you saying. But on one of the many (most!) days of my life while juggling home, work, board meetings, and all the other duties of my multi-tasking life, a good friend—a health care professional—offered this small strategy.

"Once a day," she said, "take a 5-minute time-out and just lie flat on the floor. Close your eyes, totally relax, and let every part of your body make contact with the floor." Sound crazy? Maybe. But let me tell you, there are days when those 5-minute lie-downs are as refreshing as an afternoon at the beach. Just that one small, intentional action keeps me sane, lowers the stress, and re-centers me for the rest of my day.

It can be so easy, so why not get started? What big thing are you working on? What have you been longing to accomplish that just never seems to happen? Now, what simple action can you incorporate into your life toward that? Be honest. Ask yourself: what's the smallest step you can take—your own "no brainer"? Choose one thing you know you can and WILL do and commit to it on a regular basis. Write it down, keep track, and at the end of 28 days see what progress you've made.

Every day—often without realizing it—we dismiss small things as meaningless. But remember that classic Q & A: "How do you 'eat an elephant'? One bite at a time!" Maybe you'll find that less really IS more.

 Kyle Young has enjoyed a long career of inspiring others, creating award-winning marketing campaigns, and mentoring entrepreneurs as they birth and grow their ideas . . . one small step at a time. Find Kyle blogging at **www.Multi-TaskingWoman.com** and sharing **www.EffectiveIdeas.com** for business and life.

Thoughts are things; they have tremendous power. Thoughts of doubt and fear are pathways to failure. When you conquer negative attitudes of doubt and fear you conquer failure. Thoughts crystallize into habit and habit solidifies into circumstances.

~ Bryan Adams

Day 4

Today, I choose a thought of
Random Acts of Kindness

by Andy Greider

In a world that is busier than we've ever known—with many of us pushing the envelope each day and overcommitted to work, to family, to just about everything but sleep—committing random acts of kindness becomes more of a conscious effort in our daily lives. In fact, for many, it has been lost entirely. Yet, I'd argue there has never been a more important time in our existence than now to revive this idea.

Why am I advocating random acts of kindness?

Have you ever seen what a random act of kindness can do for someone's day?

The smile it can bring or the simple look of thanks on someone's face? Something done to help someone, out of the blue, revolutionizes their day, their week, their month, and sometimes their world. Am I being too grandiose? Perhaps on the last mention, but you never really know how your unanticipated, unasked for assistance will affect someone else's reality.

Regardless of reaction, we should always give without expecting to receive, reach out and help without some expectation of reward or return. Our world has lost some of the selflessness of past sets of generations, and unless we consciously begin to correct that we will slide further from this ideal.

Did you ever stop to think that if each person did one random act of kindness each month we could bring the world together as one people?

This one takes some imagination and some speculation. However, if every single person—regardless of gender, race, social standing, situation, or mindset at the time—took the time to commit a random act of kindness once a month, it would make the world a better place. Because this no longer is just about doing something nice; it is now about bringing people together, people from all different walks of life. Random acts of kindness help us all come to the same level, to realize we are people of the same blood and bones, and care about each other.

When we take the time to do something unrequested to help someone else, it brings us all closer together. Spend a little time assisting someone you weren't required to help and perhaps you'll see their opinion of you change. The positive effect you have might not be something you see. It may come later, when the recipient is at home and they pay that kindness forward to their spouse or child or neighbor. Each act of kindness increases exponentially thanks to the ripples it makes in otherwise still water.

When you commit a random act of kindness, you provide a spark for someone else's day AND your own.

You do, really, truly, absolutely. Not only does the person you are assisting get a boost, you do as well. From simple acts like helping someone carry a bag to their car at the grocery store, to more involved acts, like spending an evening you didn't expect to at a homeless shelter helping out, you can affect the lives of many others in a positive way. Putting someone else's needs ahead of your own agenda and doing something to help really makes you feel good. Honest. Try it. It won't hurt you, and unless you are the very rare exception, the other person won't be the only one feeling very good.

As a "warning," committing random acts of kindness is addictive. Once you start doing so, it becomes harder to stop and you're more likely to commit them more often. This leads to more people paying it forward and more people coming closer together.

Random acts of kindness help remind us that we are always able to help someone else, no matter our current situation.

No matter how well we are doing or how poorly, we can always find a way to help others with one small act of kindness. Even if you're down on your luck, you can hold a door, help a stranger with directions, or spend some time volunteering your energy to others who need even more help than you. We all get caught up in being "too busy" or convince ourselves that we're not able to be of benefit to others. In both cases, this is simply untrue. We're just not focusing on the things that will bring balance to our lives or allow us to break free of depression or increase our sense of self-worth.

We should do this to teach our children well and return what we have been given.

As I mentioned earlier, we're sliding more and more into a world where we are not teaching our next generations how to be kind to one another in a consistent, daily fashion. We are not returning the example that the generations before us set. We really can return our world to the "traditional values" and "family values" so many people purport to covet.

It begins with bringing forward that inner ability to help each other. I've heard myriad people say that this isn't possible anymore in our busy society. To that I ask you to look at how people pulled together after Katrina, after Sandy, after world tragedies—all working to help others who were less fortunate with infinite acts of random kindness. We are not only capable of it but we are in need of it as a society and not just after tragedy. Helping others because it is the right thing to do is the best way to get back to where it all begins.

So, good, you're ready to jump in. Now, what are some examples of random acts of kindness?

Rather than make a list, let's just say that if it is something you didn't HAVE to do, or something you ADDED to someone's day without thinking of yourself first, it was likely a random act of kindness. Go out and commit one—TODAY!

Andy "Google Me" Greider is a business consultant, author, radio host, and speaker, and the founder of Robin Hood Business Growth. He leverages his experience and network to help companies grow at no direct cost to them. Learn more at:
www.robinhoodbusinessgrowth.com

Day 5

Today, I choose a thought of

Inspiration

by Patricia Hayes

There is one mind common to all individual men. Every man is an inlet to the same and to all of the same. He that is once admitted to the right of reason is made a freeman of the whole estate. What Plato has thought, he may think; what a saint has felt, he may feel; what at any time has befallen any man, he can understand. Who hath access to this universal mind is a party to all that is or can be done. ~ Ralph Waldo Emerson

Inspiration comes from the latin word *inspirare*, "to breathe into," and refers to an unconscious burst of creativity. The Greeks believed that inspiration came from the gods. It is a divine matter in Hebrew poetics, and in Christianity, inspiration is a gift of the Holy Spirit.

We have all mysteriously lifted the cloud of unknowing and entered this space of no resistance and unlimited possibilities. We knew when it was happening that it was beyond our everyday thinking. Our creative expression was simply flowing through us effortlessly without a thought of time. We knew we were inspired and loved what we were doing. Emerson tells us that inspiration is the natural state of our higher and universal mind. Wouldn't it be wonderful to find a key that would take us to our universal mind whenever we desired? The perfect idea would flow through at the exact right time that it was needed. Each time I thought I found it, it was gone when I tried to use it, until one day I began searching for something else and forgot all about the Inspiration Key.

There is more to life than increasing its speed.

~ Mahatma Ghandi

Today, I will do something out of the ordinary

Sometimes we have to do something out of the ordinary to feel inspiration. Nature calls us when we need healing, and the woods and ocean call me periodically. Only this time I felt a sense of urgency and deep purpose that I hadn't felt before. I was searching for myself. Who am I? Why am I here? Is there anything more to life? Do I have a purpose other than being a daughter, wife, and mother? I felt family was extremely important but I still wanted to know if I had a purpose beyond this. I began my new search in the woods and ended up discovering the key that would unlock the mysteries of me and living an inspired life.

Nature has its own unique nourishment and wisdom to share. Nature expresses its wholeness. We all have a natural affinity with Nature that we don't seem to have with people. We see the beauty in its torn and tattered leaves. Unlike people, we don't judge its broken limbs and branches. We accept its imperfections and enjoy it exactly like it is, and Nature accepts and embraces us exactly as we are with all our imperfections. There is a sacred unity between human beings, the inspirational, intuitional, and Nature. There is a difference between the fascinating things that call us in Nature and the things we experience in our daily life and commercial world.

Most of us go about our daily life on the expressway as if we were on a single track. We know what we need to do and we set out to do it. This involves doing many different things in a day—physically working, finishing a project at work, following a diet, being stuck in traffic as we drive to our various destinations, exercising, grocery shopping, or going to a meeting. We are experts at multi-tasking and if we're not focused on a specific and particular thing to do, our awareness has a tendency to shrink. We ignore ideas and sights that call alluringly from other directions, urging us to pause and explore them. The momentary inspirations we do get seem to fade in the responsibilities of life as quickly as they appeared.

We hear the call of Nature and tell ourselves that we're too busy or the things that are calling are simply distractions that will take us away from the important things. We ignore the call from our higher self and the inspirations from the universal mind that are attempting to flow through us. We are too busy going about our routines.

When we are with Mother Nature we are in touch with aspects of ourselves that aren't often available.

- Our intuition and ability to be intimate increases.

- We receive sudden insights of what we must do.

- Our heart expands, we become aware of our Spirit, and there is a greater awareness and appreciation of our loved ones.

When we feel purpose in something grander than merely getting something done and routine achievements, we mysteriously discover interesting new aspects of self. We discover creative abilities we didn't even know we had and ways to share them. My spiritual quest to know self acted to guide me to Nature and open my bruised ego to the possibility of my higher self and the many insights and synergistic events that followed. When I realized that I was more important than anything that I did, I touched my Spirit and began living an inspired life.

Living an inspired life is finding your own unique abilities and expressing them as only you can. Do something out of the ordinary today that will inspire your own unique path to creative expression and sharing your inspirations. Inspiration is continually fueled through your desire to share what you love and know with others. Remember that inspiration is best found when you're alone with Mother Nature. With that purpose in mind, find a magical place whether it's a park, forest, stream, or a tree in your yard. Imagine yourself opening a new doorway in your life. Enter knowing that you will expand your awareness and let the coincidences, synergistic events, and insights surprise you and touch your heart. Interact with what happens on both an inner and external level. Be sure to journal your thoughts and experiences.

The revelations we receive in Nature are so direct and intimate, and so timely, we are appreciative of everything we receive. There is always excitement, uncertainty, challenge, and extreme joy in the journey of unearthing a new creative aspect of self. Trust and Know that you will give birth to a stream of inspiration and continual creative expression.

INSPIRATIONAL AFFIRMATION
I am at the right place at the right time for the right reason.

Patricia Hayes is an artist and author of five books and has appeared on numerous television programs including *A Current Affair*. She has been a pioneer in intuitive and spiritual development for 45 years and is known for her innovative teaching methods. Patricia is the founder of Delphi University in McCaysville, Georgia. **www.delphiu.com**

Day 6

Today, I choose a thought of
Self-Confidence

by Martha Forlines

The truth is self-confidence comes from repeated successes. Think about that. Is it true for you? If you are not confident and do not believe in yourself, then it is difficult for other people to believe or have confidence in you. Self-confidence helps you to be happier, more successful, perform better at work, and maintain healthy relationships at work and in your personal life. Besides that, people like to be around confident people. It shows!

How are you showing up?

What is your body language saying about you and your confidence? Be aware of these things that can make you appear less confident:

1. A weak handshake
2. Invading other people's personal space
3. Crossing your arms in front of you
4. Playing with your hair or finger nails
5. Bad posture, slumped shoulders
6. Failing to make effective eye contact
7. Appearing like you're not interested
8. Not smiling

9. Fidgeting
10. Hiding your hands

Remember, your body language speaks volumes without you saying a word.

How are you talking to yourself?

What are you saying to yourself? **Negative self talk** is that little voice in your ear trying to convince you, "I can't do this." Women say 3 times more words a day than men, on average. So as a result, women are 3 times more likely to say negative things to and about themselves!

Listen to what you are saying to yourself. Is it true? Only to you. TIPS: Raise your self-awareness of that voice in your head and understand what is causing your self-doubt. Then stop yourself. What can you do to prevent this from happening again? Come up with a short restatement of what happened, then say 3 positive, affirming things to yourself.

How are you communicating with others?

What about what you are saying to others? 3 seconds . . . that's all the time it takes to make that first impression! Think about how first impressions are made today—introductions via email, posts on your social media of choice, your resume, webinars, teleconferences—all involving your written and spoken words. All of this represents your voice. Who you are. Your brand.

There are several ways we communicate that diminish our power and perceived confidence:

1. When we speak powerfully, we think we might come across as less likeable, so we make disclaimers like, "I'm not an expert in this, but . . ."

2. Overuse of the word "just." "I just think . . ." or "I'm just concerned about . . ." These statements undermine whatever brilliant point you offer after the word "just."

3. Turning powerful statements into questions when spoken. This is referred to as uptalk. Raising your voice pitch at the end of a sentence diminishes confident verbal communications.

4. Writing rambling, run-on sentences or not pausing between sentences in a conversation. You can easily lose your reader/listener. Be thoughtful about your main message; choose your words wisely and pause.

Practice, practice, practice

Self-confidence for most of us comes as a result of repeated successes. Solving confidence issues by learning new skills and practicing them is a standard and easy solution for many people! Practice helps your confidence replace self-doubt.

So, how much do you practice? Do you feel very prepared but still don't feel confident? Read on . . .

Know thyself. ~ Socrates

Knowing yourself means knowing your own values, beliefs, fears, passions, and purpose. Truly understanding and accepting yourself is at the heart of being self-confident.

1. Your values and beliefs ground you and drive your behavior day to day, both consciously and subconsciously.

2. Your fears demean your confidence and wreak havoc with being all you desire to be. We all have them. Gaining confidence means knowing what your fears are and understanding how they are getting in your way.

Our deepest fear is that we are powerful beyond measure. It is our light, not our darkness that frightens us most.
~ Marianne Williamson

3. What is it that makes your heart sing, that will lead you to your passions and purpose? Each of us has special

gifts. You love using these gifts and feel totally confident about expressing them!

4. So, what's the solution, you ask? Gaining a deeper understanding of yourself. Knowing what causes your confidence to come and go is a necessary step in holding onto your confidence when you need it the most.

Trust Yourself

Do you choose to trust yourself? The word for trust in French is "confiance." Sounds a lot like "confidence," doesn't it? To better understand this relationship, read this quote from Rachel Naddor:

> Self-confidence comes from self-trust. We feel confident when we listen to our own inner guidance, our intuition. We make the best decisions when we still our mind, get introspective and ask ourselves, "What is the best choice for me . . . what feels right for me?"

Listening to what everybody else thinks can make you crazy. Listen to what your intuition is telling you. Trust yourself!

Love Yourself

Patrice Dickey, a wise author, explained further that there are four pillars of a happier, more confident life:

1. Be more self-aware—of yourself and your impact on others in your life. "Self observation is a vital habit."

2. The hallmark of high self-confidence is self-acceptance. That's right, accepting your strengths and accepting your limitations.

3. Having self-respect. Yes, respect for yourself is essential to gaining self-confidence.

4. Love thyself is the last and most important of the four pillars.

Think about it this way. When you can achieve these four important elements to become more self-confident and happy, you naturally will project or transfer awareness, acceptance, respect, and love to others in your life. Which of these four pillars do you need to focus on the most?

We've talked about tips and tools for you to get and keep your self-confidence to create repeated successes for yourself everyday:

1. Raising your self-awareness of how you are showing up, nonverbally and verbally;

2. What you are saying to yourself;

3. How you are saying things to others;

4. How practice and preparedness can keep you on track; and

5. The essence of self-confidence—your relationship with yourself.

Consciously get to know yourself, then move from self-acceptance to self-respect and ultimately to self-love. This last step enables self-confidence and confidence in your relationships with others.

Martha Forlines is a nationally known executive coach, employee engagement and performance consultant, speaker, and author of *Inspiring Women: BECOMING Courageous, Wise Leaders*. She has over 30 years of results-oriented business experience to enable her clients to get the results they desire. **www.beliefsysteminstitute.com**

We can complain because rose bushes have thorns, or rejoice because thorn bushes have roses.

~ Abraham Lincoln

Day 7

Today, I choose a thought of
Flexibility

by Sandy Weaver Carman

Did you wake up this morning feeling stiff? No, I don't mean your joints, I mean your outlook.

As humans, we are hard-wired to value the status quo: the job we have, the partner we have, the house we have, and all the other "haves" that we have. We work to have more, certainly, but we expect, at the end of each day, that we will continue to have all of our "haves" and that those things will make us happy.

I know, some days your job doesn't make you very happy, but the paycheck usually does. Some days your spouse might not make you very happy, but those days are outnumbered by good ones. Some days you might want to push your car off a cliff, but you keep it until an infatuation with a newer one forces a change.

As humans, we value the things we have more highly than those we don't, and by placing a high value on them, we often miss something that would suit us even better.

An odd thing happens when we try to hold on to what we value—the tighter the grip, the less happy the object of our desire makes us. Keeping it means work and stress and the possibility of loss! And we get so busy focusing on maintaining control that we forget why we valued those things in the first place.

You probably think I'm going to suggest getting rid of a lot of the things you value, and you can do that if you'd like. Many life coaches use a "paring down" approach very successfully with their clients, and I'm not going to argue with success.

But I'm going to suggest something a bit different, maybe even a little bit radical. All of the people and things in your life are there for a reason. Think about the reason for each: the reason you chose your partner in life, the reason you chose your house, the reason you work where you do, the reason you have all the things you value. One by one, think about each, and if a smile comes to your lips, then there is still value there for you, and you should probably hold on.

But be flexible, and by that I mean don't hold on like your life depends on it, because it doesn't. Your life depends on your next heartbeat, your next breath, and your ability to acquire food and water. Your life depends on nothing—and no one—else.

Being flexible means that you love your partner, but you understand you do not control your partner. Some traits may drive you up a wall, but you have to allow for individuality, moodiness and even eccentricities.

Being flexible means you do the best you can do at your job and hope you can be there for a long time, but you can cope if cutbacks happen.

Being flexible means you enjoy your car and take care of it, but you can cope if it gives up the automotive ghost.

Being flexible means you surround yourself with things you love in your home, but you won't shrivel up and die if a catastrophe happens.

Sometimes being flexible is harder than others. My husband and I faced that not too long ago with the death of one of our dogs. She was old, to be sure, but seemed to be in excellent health.

Her last day was delightful—she ran around the yard, head and tail held high, enjoying the smells blowing in on the breeze. She ate well, played with our other two dogs, and went to bed when I did. Forty-five minutes later, when my husband came into the room, he realized she was gone.

Our hearts felt stiff. We argued with death—how could she be gone so suddenly after such a great day? We pushed against death—her birthday was the next day and we had a cake ordered. Finally, we found our flexibility and accepted her death. She didn't want to be 14, and we had to honor her choice.

When you choose a thought of flexibility, you keep your options and your heart open. More peace flows through you, and more opportunities flow to you. Or maybe it just seems that way, because you're able to recognize those opportunities. You're not working so hard to keep control over what you already have.

Today, I choose a thought of flexibility. And that thought gives my heart, soul, and imagination permission to soar!

Sandy Weaver Carman partners with writers, speakers, trainers, and coaches, taking work they've already done and turning it into a revenue river. She is CEO of Voicework on Demand, Inc., an audio production company, specializing in audio books and products. **www.voiceworkondemand.com**

By choosing your thoughts, and by selecting which emotional currents you will release and which you will reinforce, you determine the quality of your Light. You determine the effects that you will have upon others, and the nature of the experiences of your life. ~ Gary Zukav

Day 8

Today, I choose a thought of
Wisdom

by Tricia Molloy

You don't have to know all the answers; you just need to know where to look. And often the place to look is inside. There are many ways to tap into your wisdom, that inner guidance to help you co-create everything you desire. Here are three proven strategies that will help you make better decisions, solve problems easier, and support you to live a life of peace, joy, and grace.

Meditation 101

It is said that praying is talking to God and meditating is listening to God. You might think that sitting still, going within, and listening would be fairly easy to do. For many of us, it can be one of the most challenging activities we will ever endeavor. If you imagine someone wrapped in robes sitting cross-legged on a mountaintop, the process only gets more difficult.

Even the word can be intimidating. I choose to say "checking in" instead. Whatever you call it or however you get there, you'll find that this ancient Eastern custom will help you relax, put things in perspective, and gain remarkable insights. You may choose to meditate first thing in the morning or before you go to sleep. While you can consult many superb books and CDs to learn about meditation, like Jon Kabat-Zinn's *Wherever You Go, There You Are* and Jack Kornfield's *Meditation for Beginners,* I will share a few tips that have worked for me. First, remember there is no one right way to meditate. By experimenting, you will find the way that's right for you.

Let's begin. Sit comfortably with your spine straight. Keep your hands palms upward on your legs as a sign of receptivity. Think of them as small satellite dishes tuning into the universe. Pay special attention to your breath to clear your mind and connect with the infinite intelligence. Breathe fully from your diaphragm and experiment with different counts. Try breathing in for a count of three, holding for a count of four, and breathing out for a count of six. Establish a rhythm so you can soon stop counting.

At the beginning of meditation, some people prefer using a mantra they say to themselves in rhythm with their breathing. Yours may be "All is well," "I am open to receive," "Thank you, Spirit," or "Om," which rhymes with "home." Om is said to be the sound of the creation of the universe and is considered the most powerful of all mantras. Sages claim that the vibration it produces— as you maintain the sound with your outward breath—puts you in touch with the wisdom of the universe. It slows down the breathing, calms the nervous system, and gives your body's glands and organs a vibrational massage.

Stop judging your initial inability to get still. We all have constant chatter in our minds. Each time a thought pops into your head, acknowledge it and release it like a bubble that floats away. The time of stillness will increase as the thoughts decrease. I promise you that.

Go with Your Gut

Do you trust your intuition? The last time you found yourself in a situation that "felt" totally right or completely wrong, did you respect those feelings and respond accordingly?

It's that first impression you have of a prospective client at a networking event. It's that small voice that tells you to delay your hiring decision until the candidate's final reference calls back. It's that figurative "red flag" you see when the promises of an ambitious new vendor seem too good to be true. It's what helps you capitalize on a time-sensitive opportunity where, if you were to wait for all the facts to come in, it would be too late.

Tap into your sixth sense by simply asking. Let's say you are trying to decide whether to offer a new service, expand into a new market, or end a frustrating client relationship. Ask yourself how you feel if you were to do it and monitor your physical reaction. Do a "gut check." Has your breath become shallow and are your muscles a little tighter? Or are you relaxed and loose? Now, repeat that observation as if you were to decide not to do it.

Keep track of decisions you make based on your hunches or gut feelings and check the results. As your success rate increases, you will be more likely to trust your instincts.

To Sleep, Perchance to Dream

Pulitzer and Nobel Prize-winning novelist John Steinbeck achieved worldwide recognition for his keen observations and powerful descriptions of the human condition. The author of *The Grapes of Wrath* once said, "It is a common experience that a problem difficult at night is resolved in the morning after the committee of sleep has worked on it."

Many prominent artists, like surrealist painter Salvador Dali and musician Paul McCartney, have attributed the source of their creations to dreams. So did Albert Einstein. According to the International Association for the Study of Dreams, a nonprofit organization dedicated to investigating this phenomenon, dreams are useful in learning more about the dreamer's feelings, thoughts, behavior, motives, and values. Dreams can help solve problems and enhance your creativity.

Are you trying to write a compelling sales letter, choose new software, or effectively reward your top producers? Why don't you summon "the committee of sleep"? Start by clearing your mind of distractions. Refrain from watching television or reading that evening. Take a moment to decide what problem you want to solve and write it down. Visualize yourself dreaming about the problem. You may even choose to add some symbolic items to your bed table. Or you could draw the result, like a group of happy clients. When you write down your dreams, don't get discouraged if they don't quite make sense. Keep a dream diary. It may take time before that "light bulb" goes off and you understand the connection between the images or scenarios and your solution.

To thinking with wisdom!

Through employee development programs and conference keynotes, **Tricia Molloy** inspires professionals to achieve their goals faster and easier by using wise business practices. She is an engaging motivational speaker and the author of *Working with Wisdom: 10 Universal Principles for Enlightened Entrepreneurs.*
www.triciamolloy.com

Day 9

Today, I choose a thought of
Balance

by Ginnie Faye Liman

I'm sure the very word balance conjures up a vision of some costumed juggler, full of fun and frolic, splaying both feet on a barrel board while flipping jugs in midair.

To be sure, balancing on objects takes talent, but here I'm referring to a different sort of balance not restricted to acrobatics. The balance I speak of is wholistic, it's man seeking it as a blessing. It is a release for the soul, giving it complete expression. It gives the body a voice that tells you how it feels and what it needs from you to be happy. Synergistically, it grounds the body to the earth and yet it feels like you are floating. It quiets the mind with waves of soft energy which permeate delightfully from the spirit. It is a place where soul, body, and intellect can meet divinely. Balance in its best sense renews, restores, and replenishes.

The conditions affecting balance change daily. Balance will not unfold the same way every day. It may be circuitous, for one day the body may be more tired than the day before. The environment may vary, so might weather conditions. As such, balance needs to "establish" itself anew every day. What do I mean by that? Surely you say that can't be right when there are concepts like "balance the books, balance on a beam, balance one's checkbook, a balance of trade, a balanced diet."

Even on a balance beam you see a gymnast adjust her balance. Each day the conditions are different. As observed in the Olympics, there is no certainty when it comes to balance. A balanced diet becomes unbalanced at the first chocolate indulgence. To be sure there are perfect moments, but they are rare and involve either the mind, the body, or the spirit individually. That is why balance must be practiced regularly. To master balance takes patience, dedication, and commitment. But the reward is a whole new level of mastery.

Balance is a place where the soul, body, and intellect can meet divinely. Balance is a state so enmeshed and so intrinsic that every day becomes a graceful unfolding. It is the harmony of body, mind, and spirit working with perfect synchronicity in an even flowing state.

The great gurus and inspirational masters of meditation have achieved it. Yogis, monks, and the great contemplatives of life like Gandhi, Buddha, Lao Tzu, and Kahil Gibran, were the extraordinary thinkers and geniuses who so inspire us. In modern times we think of the Dalai Lama oppressed by the Chinese protecting Tibet and living his truth in exile. Dr. Wayne Dyer spent a lifetime on a cultural quest seeking the great secrets of life and man. Nelson Mandela, now 94, spent 27 years in prison fighting racist white rule and managed to maintain his karma through grueling trials, evidencing quiet courage and composure.

These extraordinary men encourage us to seek spiritual enlightenment, and they speak of meditation and balance as the highest order of things. All are transformational guides revealing man in his remarkability, the secrets of living fully even with great restrictions.

In 1999 a revolutionary book flew off the bookstands. Eckhart Tolle's brilliant bestseller *The Power of Now* urges us to focus our energies on empowerment, the practice of balancing one's mind by living completely in the moment. It emphasizes how the mind chooses to dominate, and when it does it, creates great imbalances in our lives. This angst, anxiety, and worry cause people to obsess.

Again "balance" is the bingo word—Tolle says the best antidote to letting the mind take over is meditative breathing. As Tolle explains, the mind is all about ego and control, not willing to give up its power or noise. It will try to deter the creation of balance. Deep breathing and full concentration should provide a fortress against distraction. Daily meditation will train the mind to calm itself as well as reinforce your commitment to balance. Cultivate it by scheduling fifteen minutes a day. Gradually increase the meditation time to train and educate the mind to the awesome advantages ahead. Eventually the mind will associate the meditation time with renewal and generate a new sense of well-being.

Any illusion that balance can be achieved through sheer will must be relinquished. Because the mind is impatient it will only listen if it is trained. As stillness is respected, revelations will rise from the spirit, and deeper insights will prevail. It will create its own enchantment. The mind will notice this.

As you faithfully follow the ebb and flow of your breath you will send a signal to the mind—*that you will not be distracted.* The spirit will be enthralled and the contentment of a balanced state will begin to emanate. The importance of balance in life is almost incalculable. *Its essence rests wholly on the concept of trust*—of self, a higher power, universal good, and the ability to yield wholeheartedly to that.

Balance cannot be feigned, forced, or aggressively sought. It is the epiphany that reveals itself as the wisdom uttered by the greats.

Balance requires us to be an acute observer of life, leading down the pathway of cosmic consciousness.

Balance begins with awareness, diving deeply, noticing fleeting emotions and witnessing events.

It requests you be in rhythm with the time, the place, the outcome.

Balance is the melting point between bitter and sweet.

Balance is the merging of yin and yang.

Balance is a splotch of white on black.

Balance is the nuance of assertion.

Balance is bounty overcoming scarcity.

Balance is the meeting place between finite and gargantuan.

Balance is holding judgments in abeyance.

Balance is welcoming, yet detached.

Balance is a state of evenness . . . a harmony of two coexisting states. *Balance* is the mingling of hot and cold . . . meeting at lukewarm. *Balance* is everything.

This is the Beneficence of Balance.

From early childhood **Ginnie Faye Liman** has been in love with words, drawn to the harmony of sounds letters would make, fascinated when words were put to music and they would coalesce. Loving the artistry of writing, she reflects on life's ambiguities to bring new ideas to the fore. **gliman@bellsouth.net**

Day 10

Today, I choose a thought of

Life's STORY, a play

by Kathryn Sener

NOW SHOWING:

Sometimes you don't know which end is up, but when you think about it in the form of a play, there is always a happy ending!

~~~

Talent in Life's STORY, a play program:

Life's STORY, a play

Our Lord, Jesus Christ, Featured Artist

Master teacher, author of salvation, provider of the God-breathed book known as the Bible and creator of your talents, knowing every move you make and every hair on your head, all you will need, your everything!

You and I, Featured Artists

We are masters of many God-given talents featuring competency in all we do to make sure our play scores the highest ratings based on the developed talents. Mine are themed presenter, production consultant, writer, creative leader, and teacher.

What are your Featured Artistic Attributes and Talents?

Also Featuring:

Relationships, people, and places playing a significant role in our attitude. Hobbies, past roles, your confidence, boldness, or reservedness, communicative style, passion, and mission reveal whom you will feature in your Story.

A creative spirit, leader, mentor, or muse can spark a song to the heart, a restoration to the soul of what is important to you and the people you serve.

Who are you featuring?

Who are your supporting role players or models?

Produced By YOU:

I am the producer of each day and blessed to be given free control of making decisions. I love to tell the story and live the story not only of my life but also of many others. My hope is to make the fairy tale come to life. Fortunately, I have been given that beautiful script by realizing the value of each day.

What are you producing?

~~~

Stage Setting:

The purpose of this thought, your story, is to help you reflect, for a moment, on the direction of the story you are producing. Is it where you want to be? Who you want to be? Does your stage really reflect where you want to play?

Scenario:

Restoration, Perspective, Movement, and Props are what you (person and/or company) need to make the story come alive with who you are. Participate in your Story, whether short and simple or long and determined, reflecting on the God-given blessings and giving thanks through daily praise. It is not all easy, but the hard stuff happens behind the stage curtain, not on stage.

Finale

Write it and finish it well. Everyone has one, a story, that is. You create stories every hour of the day; the crescendo is your awareness of the grace given to you to perform. Now go break a leg!

Thanks for acting it out!

You Only Live Once:

Live It Well, Tell It Well, and Ride it with Full Enjoyment with your God-given Grace.

~~~

Journeys:

Recently I moved from a home I had been in for 17 years. While packing, I reflected on life's journey thru these rooms from

Make each day reflect your ENCORE

the art on the walls to the sidetracking of picture albums of family and friend gatherings. Life is a traveling storybook of blessings when you look for them. Why not make each day reflect your ENCORE, when you say "thank you" for the opportunity!

Contributors:

"No man is an island." ~ John Donne

"Success is where preparation and opportunity meet." ~ Bobby Unser

"If God is for us who can be against us?" ~ Romans 8:31

All sound familiar?

Contributors:

There are many supporters in business and in life that play a part to who we are and who we will become. My contributor is my faith in Christ for forgiveness of all my crazy mistakes and the courage to accept forgiveness and get back up, my family for always being there, and my friends who stick by me and tell me I am the best even when I have my doubts.

Who are your contributors?

Thanks To:

Where does one begin? The key is using the words "Thank You" and using them every day. Thank You for the awakening of a new day, a new hour, a new perspective, a new way to look at something old.

My thanks goes to the same contributors mentioned above, but also to the beauty that surrounds me (I love gardens and nature); my best friend, Steve, who has given me a new way to look at some hidden creative talents; and the confidence to make something of it.

Who deserves your thanks today?

Kathryn Sener is a stage producer for products, people, and businesses; a resource and relationship builder; mentor; creative leader thru the arts of photography and writing; and enthusiast for showing the positive aspects of a business through the eventful presentation of simplicity in a story. She leverages nearly 30 years of successful new market entry with attune-ness to clients' needs to support the stage of market growth with creativity, sales, management, and product development. **www.knewstage.com**

Today, I choose a thought of
A Peaceful Home

by Betty Humphrey Fowler

He is happiest, be he king or peasant, who finds peace in his home.
~ Johann Wolfgang von Goethe

Our homes should be our safe havens—welcoming and supporting us every time we return from being out in the world. We should feel safe and protected and be able to rest, rejuvenate, and reconnect with ourselves and our loved ones. The more we can create a feeling of peace and happiness in our homes, the better our homes will support peace and happiness in our lives.

When you walk into your home, are you greeted by fresh flowers, clean countertops, and art that you love on the walls, or do you see clutter, unfinished projects, messy counters, and generic décor that doesn't have any meaning?

A peaceful home reduces stress triggers and can help its occupants heal from physical and emotional wounds. I learned this firsthand when my husband, a career police officer, developed an acute case of Post-Traumatic Stress Disorder (PTSD). Working at a job that regularly handles conflict, destruction, and death takes its toll on a person. One proverbial straw on the camel's back can push someone into a deep, dark place of despair. When that happened to my husband, the only thing I felt I had control over was our home environment where he was spending all of his time.

Following basic Feng Shui principles, I removed items in our home that did not support a peaceful space for him to heal—sickly looking plants, the pile of outdated magazines haphazardly tossed on the floor in the living room, the dust bunnies in the corners, and paper clutter on the kitchen table. The entire house was kept as clean and organized as possible. Beds were made as soon as we got up, dishes were put in the dishwasher immediately after use, and healthy plants were placed in the living room and kitchen. Brighter colors were brought into our spaces to balance out the energy and keep it uplifted. Relaxing music and light reading replaced our standard habit of watching the news or suspenseful action shows on TV prior to bedtime. After we made all of these changes in our home, there was a peace and calm we had never felt before,  which helped all of us deal better with the ups and downs of going through such an emotional situation.

If you would like to create a more peaceful home, here is a quick list of changes you can implement.

Open your space and give yourself room to breathe.

Our possessions are a reflection of how we identify ourselves in the world. Holding onto more than we can use or honor begins to clutter and congest our homes. Just like our physical bodies, when congestion occurs in our physical spaces, life energy (or chi) cannot circulate freely and becomes stagnant. Our homes then become dis-eased. When we release the clutter and keep our physical spaces clean and open, fresh air can flow freely and we can breathe deeply. We then become more at ease and at peace in our homes.

Repair what is not working.

Squeaky door hinges, loose doorknobs, burned-out light bulbs, and cracked windows and mirrors reflect back to us that something is not working properly—we aren't able to get a handle on life or see new opportunities being presented. If something can't be repaired, it needs to be removed from the environment.

Let the light shine in.

Sunshine is a primary life-giving element. Allow as much natural light into your home as you can. When that is not possible, substitute with full-spectrum light bulbs, candles, oil lamps, or other light-producing items. Light creates a feeling of warmth and positive energy in your home and heart.

Bring nature into your home.

There are so many man-made materials surrounding us—polyester/nylon carpeting, laminate counters, chemically treated upholstery fabrics and foam, as well as electric appliances, computers, and TVs. When a lot of our time is spent indoors, we lose touch with nature and can feel irritable, out of balance, and ungrounded. It is important to bring items into our homes that reconnect us with nature.

Healthy, live plants have a two-fold benefit in our homes. Not only do they bring life into a space, they reduce toxins in the air. One easy-to-care-for favorite is the Peace Lily (and what better way to literally bring more peace into your home)! Fresh flowers, table top fountains, and aquariums also bring in life energy to areas such as a family room, dining room, or kitchen. You can also add artwork depicting natural landscapes or animals. For calmer forms of décor to use in bathrooms and bedrooms, where rest and relaxation are a priority, an orchid plant or a bowl of fresh water with river rocks and floating flowers can be added.

Create a peaceful bedroom.

Skin tone wall colors, from cream to cocoa, create a welcoming space to relax and rejuvenate your energy. Only items that give you a feeling of love and support should be allowed in this room. This means that workout equipment, office desks, and televisions are not part of the décor! If there is no other place for them in the home, cover them before going to sleep so their active energy won't keep you from getting a good night's sleep.

These five suggestions may seem simple, but sometimes they are not easy to do, especially when it involves letting go. If you hold the thought that changing your home's energy will improve the quality of your life, these small steps won't feel so difficult. Choosing the thought of a peaceful home will bring you one step closer to a peaceful life.

Betty Humphrey Fowler is a Feng Shui Consultant and Certified Interior Re-Designer. She has been helping people transform their lives by improving the energy flow of their homes and work spaces for over 12 years. **www.feelgoodinyourspace.com**

Day 12

Today, I choose a thought of
Legacy

by Jim Hogan

So often in our daily lives we never look far enough into the future to see the greatness that we will become, the lives we touch during the journey we call life, the love we share, and the inspiration we offer to others. So, today I choose a thought of legacy and the wonderment of what I will leave behind.

Every day that you wake, you add one puzzle piece to your own legacy. Your life's puzzle is infinitely large and at the same time is extremely close to being finished. You just don't know how close to completion you are. The challenge in building your own life's puzzle is that you don't have a finished photo on the puzzle box to help you place the pieces and complete the picture as designed. You create your life; you paint the picture as you go.

There are times that the picture is so clear and the choices you make are easy. Other times it feels as if you are floating in a ship off the coast of Nova Scotia in a thick fog bank, hoping that you don't steer the ship into the rocks and you hesitate or fail to act at all.

Go confidently in the direction of your dreams. Live the life you've imagined. ~ Henry David Thoreau

Who comes to mind when you think of someone who has left his or her own mark on the world? Maybe Abraham Lincoln, Ronald

Reagan, or Mother Theresa? Maybe Steve Jobs, Ted Turner, Jack Welch, or Michael Gerber? In reality, you don't have to be a world leader to have impacted the world in some way because your legacy is important to those around you whether you know it or not.

Who impacted your life in a way that you will honor them by carrying their legacy onward? For me there were a few: Mrs. Mitchell, a very special teacher who saw something in me that no one else saw and sparked a love for the outdoors,; Coach Foreman who helped me expand my goals and reach beyond my limitations, and Fred Sassler, the best boss I ever had who liked me from the start because my grandmother was from Hungary.

I am honored to carry the legacy of my mother, Audrey Madeline Hogan, who passed away on February 14, 2012, Valentines Day. Her legacy lives on in the hearts and minds of all who knew her. In the days following her death, her legacy became apparent as family and friends gathered, shared memories, laughed, cried, and celebrated her life.

Mom taught me the power of a smile and showed me how to bring a smile to others. If you can't already tell, I carry an optimistic outlook on life, just like Mom.

Since Mom always seemed to carry a smile, I created a game that I call "Smile, and pass it on." The goal of the game is to bring a smile to someone's face who is having a bad day. Helping someone find a reason to smile is not so hard. It may be as simple as smiling at them, a few words of encouragement, a compliment, a laugh, or maybe just bringing awareness of the sun's warmth, the warm summer wind, or the cool, crisp spring morning.

When you see a person's sour demeanor crack and the smile reveal itself, your smile becomes brighter, and you know their new-found smile will be passed on to others and the ripple effect can and will possibly travel around the world. Can you imagine our world if more people found a reason to smile each and every day? Go ahead and help someone smile today.

Building your legacy can be as simple as choosing a few traits that you want others to see in you and acting on those words. Here is a list of a few positive attributes to guide your actions and to look for in others:

Agreeable, Ambitious, Boundless, Brave, Bright, Calm, Capable, Charming, Cheerful, Confident, Cooperative, Courageous, Creative, Credible, Dashing, Dazzling, Debonair, Decisive, Delightful, Detailed, Determined, Diligent, Dynamic, Eager, Efficient, Elated, Enchanting, Encouraging, Energetic, Entertaining, Enthusiastic, Excellent, Excited, Exuberant, Fabulous, Fair, Faithful, Fantastic, Fearless, Fine, Friendly, Funny, Generous, Gentle, Glorious, Good, Happy, Harmonious, Helpful, Hilarious, Honorable, Jolly, Joyous, Kind, Kind-hearted, Knowledgeable, Likeable, Lively, Lovely, Loving, Lucky, Nice, Pleasant, Productive, Protective, Proud, Punctual, Receptive, Reflective, Resolute, Responsible, Romantic, Self-assured, Sensitive, Silly, Sincere, Skillful, Smiling, Splendid, Stimulating, Strong, Successful, Talented, Thoughtful, Thrifty, Trustworthy, Upbeat, Vivacious, Warm, Wise, Witty, Wonderful

Today, I choose to think about and live my life as I want the world to remember me when I am no longer of this world. I choose to be Helpful, Dedicated, Genuine, Supportive, Patient,

Approachable, Sincere, Kind, Strong, Passionate, Decisive, Honest, Inspired, and Creative.

So, smile and pass it on. Choose to live the legacy you dream by being the person you want to be with all of the drive and desire and passion behind your actions.

Be Your Legacy!

Jim Hogan is a trainer with the Referral Institute who speaks to companies and groups on networking, referral marketing, and leveraging social media to reach their niche market and explode sales. **www.JimHogan.net**

Day 13

Today, I choose a thought of

Love ALLways

by Cheryl Anne McGill

Comprehending the nature of God and humankind, understanding the power of the mind, and knowing how to pray will
not stimulate spiritual growth unless applied to daily living.
~ Mary L. Kupferle

For the purpose of this chapter, please use Spirit, Divine Mind, The Almighty, Father God, Mother God, Confucius, Allah, Buddha, Christ, The Creator, or any other term that resonates with you.

I have imparted thousands of messages worldwide through readings as a psychic medium, served as a vessel through which Spirit communicates, and undertaken a lifelong exploration to understand the nature of Divine Mind and humankind. From this I believe we, as Spirit with Divine Mind, decide to enter into a human body with each and every incarnation for one reason, and one reason alone. There is merely one explanation why we, lifetime after lifetime, choose to cooperate in a co-creative experience. Yes, there is one reason why we wish to increase our individual and collective vibration, and merely one reason why we desire the highest good for all. That reason is *to Love ALLways®—always, and in all ways.*

If you conduct a search online for the book *The Secret*, you will discover blog after blog written by individuals who long to share their personal tales of transformation. Story upon story point to how the writers have drawn everything they want into their lives by applying the Universal Law, the Law of Attraction. Countless believers trust that others can do the same, that everyone can live an abundance-filled life. All you have to do is co-create the experience with the Universe, and you too can live happily ever after! They say it is simple. Just envision what it is you want, and be grateful for it now, as though it is already in your life. Yet, billions endure all forms of human deprivation and worldly lack, angst, pain, and suffering. So, if we each choose to come into human form, if we choose to co-create an experience as Spirit with Divine Mind to Love ALLways, why is there immense disparity in the world? If the process of altering one's life from one of scarcity to one of abundance is so easy, why isn't everyone living an extraordinarily blissful life, and what can we do about it?

Those who suffer from the atrocities of life offer themselves and others the opportunity to love and be loved unconditionally ALLways. Our spirits graciously agree prior to birth to come into human form. The multitudes that undergo human suffering contract with all those living on the planet, and in the other dimensions, to experience pain on a large-scale level. They do that so humankind will be rendered a chance to increase our individual and collective frequency vibration. They co-create with us as Divine Mind for the higher good of all. This is a part of the Divine design. In truth it is the only plan—the plan for the betterment of all that is. There are no mistakes.

Still, does the knowledge that we reincarnate for the betterment of humankind and all that is remove our accountability to and for those that suffer? If we are our Brother's and Sister's keepers, and we wish to increase our individual and collective vibration through loving ALLways, do we have the ability to effect change? If so, how do we start?

Most want everyone to experience love and to know that love is the very essence of who we are. All the same, we believe our contributions would not make a difference to the billions endeavoring to survive. And we genuinely do not know how to begin.

I offer you a suggestion. What if I said you can make a colossal difference to those who undergo seemingly insurmountable struggles, and to all that is, yourself included, by being honest. Yes, that's it! Just be honest. Are you willing to be honest and, hence, create the life you want for yourself and others by living authentically?

Honesty is mandatory if we are to live an abundance-filled life. When we love ourselves we are honest with ourselves and with others. In truth, we actually live through and as love. We become the full expression of Divine Mind. As we live authentically, compassion for oneself and others is increased. When we are open to being compassionate, we forgive, and we accept. As we allow acceptance, we begin to love ALLways. And something else really incredible happens! We create monumental changes in our energy field. It expands and emits a higher energetic frequency—a love vibration! This love vibration is felt everywhere, and in everything since there is no separation—we are all interconnected.

Through this cooperative co-creative experience, everyone and everything is healed. The symptoms that stem from lack of love become a thing of the past. The illusion of scarcity ceases to exist with an outward manifestation of abundance of love. The same love which has been present from the conception of energy. And what's really impressive is that the increase in our love vibration causes the planetary vibration to rise and expand further into the Universe, which produces more love. Energetically, everyone and everything ascend to a higher state of being!

In closing, I envision a world in which everyone has a practice of affirmative prayer—not beseeching prayer. We meditate and commune with Divine Mind. We service others by loving ALLways.

Abundance prevails as we know that we are interconnected and of Divine Mind in unity. We engage a practice of gratitude daily and are grateful now. We know that everything that is necessary for the highest good of all to be realized is already present. The Divine design is in perfect working order. We trust that the planetary frequency is already vibrating in love. We share our personal tales of transformation and apply the Universal Law of Attraction. Miracles happen now. We co-create an experience with the Universe and are living happily ever after! And so it is, and we let it be.

Love ALLways, Cheryl Anne McGill

Cheryl Anne McGill, RN, MBA, DD, MscD, is a life-partner, mother, grandmother, internationally renowned psychic medium, medical intuitive, radio host, motivational speaker, interfaith minister, educator, author, and advocate for human and animal rights. Born a spiritual medium, Cheryl Anne has over 50 years experience conveying messages of love from those in other dimensions and educating those in body about death and dying, quantum physics, and spirituality. **www.PsychicEnterprises.com**

Day 14

Today, I choose a thought of
Forgiveness

by Kristin Colier

Forgiveness is fundamental in creating a life of inner peace and happiness. Spend today welcoming forgiving thoughts in all your interactions, at work, while running errands, and with your family. Anytime you feel upset, wronged, irritated, or mistreated, consider forgiveness.

Observe characters in movies, books, or on TV. Learn from the conflicts and confrontations these characters face. Imagine if our heroes chose to forgive rather than be tortured by the past or seek revenge. How would the story change?

Forgiveness is an Option

Holding on to anger is like drinking poison and waiting for the other person to die. ~ The Buddha

The biggest hurdle to forgiveness is in accepting it as a realistic option. Some people hold grudges and resentment as if they're a requirement of life, like battle scars or badges of honor. Consider instead that clinging to reasons you won't forgive is merely an act of "drinking poison." Rather than hurting those we refuse to forgive, we only harm ourselves.

Reasons People Do Not Forgive

- *"He doesn't deserve forgiveness."* When you realize your thoughts, actions, or feelings are being dictated by someone you dislike, you must forgive them to free yourself. What you deserve is a life untethered to the unenlightened or irresponsible actions of others.

- *"If I forgive him, he'll think his actions were acceptable."* Create boundaries or consequences if you need to protect yourself from further incidents. Talk about the issue if it's a relationship you value, but don't hold a grudge or let anger disempower you.

- *"She never said, 'I'm sorry.'"* Forgive even the most hard-hearted, unapologetic transgressors. This is how you know that the grace to forgive is yours alone.

- *"I would be letting someone down."* People are tempted to create solidarity by having a common enemy. We are often invited by others to form alliances or show allegiance by blaming others for our situation. This happens with peers and within families, but it is also at the root of religious persecution, bigotry, racism, and jingoistic patriotism. Refuse to let someone else's inability to forgive become your own.

Steps to Practice Forgiveness

1. Identify a situation, memory, or incident that angers or upsets you. Consider forgiveness as an option. Realize forgiveness is an act of freeing yourself.

2. Be conscious of any disempowering thoughts of blame, shame, or guilt around the situation.

3. Understand that the past is past; it cannot be changed. Reacting to past events in the present is your choice and

your responsibility to process and deal with. For today, blame no one else for your state of mind. Here are two useful affirmations: "I am responsible for my life." "I am responsible for my happiness."

4. Create new positive or empowering thoughts and meaning to associate with the situation.

5. Identify "trigger events" and exercise your new thought patterns.

6. Tap into your compassion. People behave in ways that affect us for all sorts of reasons: the way they were raised, their cultural or religious belief systems, they don't know any better, they had similar wrongs done to them, they have no positive role models, they have some other unseen pain that you don't know about. The reason is not important. Just recognize that we are all human and subject to the same flaws, fallibilities, and life experiences as everyone else. Other souls need healing too.

Whom to Forgive

- *Strangers.* Forgive the person who cut you off in traffic or the waitress who gave you terrible service. Release them from having any affect on your mood or your day.

- *Instigators.* Forgive the vitriolic political pundits, the Facebook commenter determined to get a rise out of you, co-workers who push your buttons. A sense of calm, forgiving, non-reaction is a gift you give yourself. It also has the benefit of removing these people from your radar. You simply stop noticing them.

- *Offenders.* These are the people who have created pivotal moments in your life that may have changed your view of the world. Maybe you have been raped, robbed, terrorized, imprisoned, or had such done to someone you love. This is hard to forget and even harder to forgive. But when you realize that years later, your thoughts, actions, moods, and emotions are being dictated by the very person you'd least like to have that power, it is necessary to let that go. Regain control. Your state of mind belongs to you and no one else.

I admit this takes work. It is my intention to simply plant the seed that forgiveness is your option in these circumstances. It is the key to creating peace of mind and a happier future that is not complicated by stories you tell yourself about the past.

- *Mom and Dad.* I'd like to think there is a statute of limitations on blaming our parents for our lot in life. (Especially now that I am a mother myself.) And while it's true that how you were raised has a lot to do with your belief system and the path you started on, your direction from here on out is entirely up to you. Chances are they did the best they could with what they knew at the time. Had they raised you differently, you'd likely be blaming them for something else. Thank them for the things they got right and say, "I'll take it from here."

- *Yourself.* Yes, we all made some big mistakes in our past. You may still feel guilt or regret about them. Feeling bad changes nothing. Your goal today is to create a future you desire, not rewrite the past. Acknowledge that you acted out of who you were then, and that today you are wiser. Try the affirmation: "I am moving toward the person I aspire to be every day. I forgive myself."

NOW WHAT?

To forgive is to set a prisoner free and discover that the prisoner was you. ~ Lewis B. Smedes

Just for today, observe life through the lens of forgiveness. Of all the great spiritual teachings and wise words I have heard, forgiveness is a fundamental and recurring attribute which leads to a life of greater peace and happiness. There are many ways to help foster forgiveness. You may visualize washing the feet of the other person, write a letter and never send it, or practice techniques such as The Sedona Method or Ho'oponopono. Once you have decided to forgive, find the practice that works for you. Today, choose a thought of forgiveness. Tomorrow, experience peace of mind.

Kristin Colier is a freelance writer, speaker, and spiritual seeker. She aspires to be a catalyst for helping others on their journey to live happier, more fulfilling lives and create a future they desire. Learn more at **www.daydreamcafe.com**.

Our life is what our thoughts make it. A man will find that as he alters his thoughts toward things and other people, things and other people will alter towards him.

~ James Allen

Day 15

Today, I choose a thought of

Movement

by Jennifer Moore

It takes a lot of courage to release the familiar and seemingly secure, to embrace the new. But there is no real security in what is no longer meaningful. There is more security in the adventurous and exciting, for in movement there is life, and in change there is power. ~ Alan Cohen

Movement is powerful, action-filled, and life-sustaining! Movement is the key to joyful life. In all things, there is a cause and effect which begins with a thought. Movement is the effect of a thought. You have a thought: I want a new job, I want health, I want a new or improved relationship. I want to know something greater in my life. Do you have everything you want? If not, this daily diet plan is for YOU!

You think, "I want a new job." Then there is a feeling, an excitement that conjures up inside your gut. Then there is space . . . What next? Do you apply for the job? Do you ask the guy/girl out? Do you go to the gym? This is where the rubber hits the road; put your money where your mouth is! Movement is essential in life. It is a catalyst to change. Movement is the breath of life; it is Prana or life force. In yoga, we learn there is a union that unites the mind and the body. Your thoughts and your movements unite you to your higher power. Movement puts you in the driver seat of your life.

The feeling of control is closely associated to movement. If you want to feel like you have more control in your life, take a step forward. Marianne Williamson teaches about empowerment. Empowerment is the feeling you have when you know you are responsible for your life. If you want to feel empowered, Williamson instructs you to do something that makes you feel powerful. I say, MOVE! Take one step forward and the universe will rise up to meet you where you are. If you want that new job, start preparing your resume or start your networking plan today. DO NOT DELAY.

We have been told that we have close to 60,000 thoughts a day and that many of these thoughts are the same ones we had yesterday. So, why not take an action step on one of your 60,000 thoughts? You will feel powerful and strong when you take charge of your life rather than sitting and waiting to be rescued by the job fairy or waiting for Santa to deliver the perfect body or relationship. Your one little movement will create a ripple effect that stirs your senses and emotions, which starts the wheels of the Law of Attraction into motion.

So if movement is great, why is it so difficult to do? Movement means change. Change creates fear. When you are living in a state of fear, you are calibrating at a low level of energy, says David Hawkins, author of *Power VS. Force: The Hidden Determinants of Human Behavior*. He explains how the levels of human consciousness change over time and has studied the range of attitudes and emotions that are localized by energy fields. An increase in your calibration can increase your power enormously. This increase starts with a thought! Just to give you an idea of what calibration looks like in a person's behavior, Jesus calibrated at 900; the motivation of Mahatma Gandhi calibrated at 700.

Hawkins states, "All levels below 200 are destructive of life in both the individual and society at large; all levels above 200 are constructive expressions of power." Fear is noted to calibrate at an energy level of 100. Fear controls many facets of the world. People fear rejection, pain, pleasure, success. Fear is a primal motivation in behavior. Fear stops movement and limits life. So, how do you overcome fear?

AWARENESS of your fears is the first step. Become consciously aware of how you sabotage your success. When and why do you stop moving in the direction of your desired goal? I am reminded of a great quote by Swami Kripalu, "The highest spiritual practice is self-observation without judgment . . . self-observation with love." Begin to observe your behaviors with compassion. Your conscious awareness is a powerful tool to empower you.

The second step is *MOVEMENT*! Take one step; activate your energy. Create a plan for the desired goal and take one step every day this week. At the end of the week you are seven steps closer to your goal.

The next step is to *TELL* three people you trust. Be mindful of whom you choose. Family can be a land mine of naysayers simply because you ignite their own fears. Consciously choose your support team to include people you respect and who want you to succeed.

The last step is to *ASK* for advice from people who have already overcome their fears. Your fears can keep you imprisoned or paralyzed. It takes a lot of energy to rise above this level, so ask other people how they achieved success. People love to tell their stories and to give advice. They will ask you how you are progressing, which holds you to a new level of integrity. Integrity to yourself is one of the highest levels of energy, because it is the truth that will set you free from your prison. It is self-love that you listen to your truth and move forward in the direction of your desires. Love calibrates at an energy level of 500. This is where you will experience joy and happiness.

When you experience true love and joy the whole world benefits. Your children are happier when you are fulfilled. Everyone around you benefits from you taking that one step. As Blaise Pascal states,

"The least movement is of importance to all nature. The entire ocean is affected by a pebble."

So, commit to yourself today to take one action step and to move in the direction of your desire and just watch the universe rise up to support you.

Jennifer Moore is a licensed clinical social worker, author, motivational speaker, and coach. She has over 15 years of experience working to move clients and organizations.
www.isisconsultingllc.com

Today, I choose a thought of
Reality Forecasting

by David Greer

Reality forecasting? What on earth? Shall we get out the crystal ball and the Ouija Board, light some candles, and work on predicting the future? Hardly. Let me explain what I mean.

On occasion, I'm one of those people who work best on a tight deadline. Seems my action impulse won't fire and my creative juices won't flow unless there is absolutely no time left in the schedule.

Yet, other times I feel like I'm in total control of my plan and then . . . wham! I end up in total chaos, scrambling at the last minute, flustered, and in an all-too-familiar state of stress. To add insult to injury, even though I'm the sole cause of my procrastinating ways and this has happened before, I actually have the audacity to be surprised! Like wow! How on earth this did this happen—again? Seriously, it's almost embarrassing that I delude myself this way.

It doesn't matter if it's Christmas shopping, packing to leave on a trip or preparing a proposal. It's the same drill. There are a few things on my mental checklist that I tend to "just accept" as dreadfully stressful. Sadly, I don't look forward to taking satisfaction from the joy in the moment or even relish the reward of completion. Instead, I hang on to the thought that "this will be over soon," and give myself the "gut it out and get through it" pep talk. Sound familiar?

Over time I've mastered the selective memory tactic. My method of dealing with these deadline-driven, chaotic event type things is to stick my head in the sand and hope things turn out differently. In fact, I've gotten so good at this I'll arrogantly add fuel to the fire by saying, "Yes," and end up taking on even more. Are you kidding me? What level of insanity exists in my psyche that propels me to do that? And like a fool, I'll once again be surprised it turned out so hard. Crazy, I know. But why is it this way?

Betcha the answer is better time management and planning, and to that I mostly agree. But wait a second. I've got the cute little day planner notepad and those neat color-coded highlighters. I have a library of self-help books and at least seven apps to make it all magically work. But somehow they don't help. True confession time—I do suppose one must actually use them to be effective.

Consequently, on my life's journeys I finally stumbled across an epiphany. It had been there all along and I suspect you have something similar tucked in your brain, as well. This simple "aha" concept is a process I refer to as *reality forecasting*.

We're smart. All of us are creatures of habit. To a person, we also have uncanny abilities to foresee circumstances with precision, gifted with an insight that allows us to predict some things with amazing accuracy. But just like those time management tools gathering dust, we can't benefit from this foresight if we don't use it to our advantage.

Back to the conundrum, but why is it this way? Think about worry. Isn't worry a fear of what's to come? Isn't it obsessing ahead of time about the reality you expect to face? Here's a brilliant thought: if we can manage to forecast reality to the point we worry, what's to stop us from using that "reality forecast" as a trigger prompting us to take early action and head off the stress in the first place?

It's too easy to live in the moment, with our focus compartmentalized into what today holds, pushing the future out of our minds. While that's not all bad—and it's a good practice in certain situations—I propose a different approach. Use a little reality forecasting to improve your performance and overall quality of life. It just may work—if you make the effort to put it in practice.

Think about the holiday season, for instance, and the preparation and decisions that come along with it. Or maybe it's a looming project deadline. Matters not if it's due in six hours, six days, six weeks, or six months. Visualize now what those hours or days will look like leading up to the momentous occasion. Paint a picture in your mind and let your imagination take you there.

What day of the week is it on? Where will you be that morning? How will the traffic be then? What other responsibilities will you have? What frame of mind will you be in? What will you wear?

I'm not suggesting that you'll get your outfit ready six months ahead, but giving thought to the patterns of behavior you've had in the past and then visualizing that reality in vivid detail is an exercise that can inspire you to be proactive versus reactive.

Don't stop with simply thinking ahead. Your perception and imagination can actually be motivation to change your course. Take a stand with yourself rather than your typical cop-out, reassuring yourself that you'll worry about it later. In other words, think in real terms and be disciplined enough to make firm mental decisions on your game plan.

Again, let's revisit the thought, but *why* is it this way? We've discussed the brilliance of actually using all the time management tools at our disposal. We've uncovered the angst of the worry factor and how to turn the tables to neutralize avoidance tendencies. Now let's consider the coup de grâce—sheer discipline.

Let's face it. Nothing is going to change unless you and I agree to change. Here's the bottom line. Decide if reality forecasting is a practice that will ease your time management, worry, and stress issues. Then put all your energy into developing a new process, checklist, or ritual that puts you firmly in the driver's seat.

David Greer is an idea practitioner and consummate storyteller. As president of Story Road, David's marketing, communications, and business development expertise is a result of his creative problem solving and visionary ideas. **www.storyroad.com**

Day 17

Today, I choose a thought of
Receiving Gracefully

by Dr. Robin Kirby

STOP!

I invite you in this moment to be fully present. Just sit, close your eyes, and notice how your body just naturally inhales and exhales bringing life-sustaining oxygen through your body. Notice the comforts that surround you NOW in THIS moment, and allow the energies of gratitude to begin to circulate in your body. This is what I call "tuning your receiver." This little exercise is essential for those who want to live in graceful receipt of all that the Universe is offering.

Just as we choose to tune our cable, radio, or satellite dish to channels that we enjoy, we owe it to ourselves to intentionally tune our conscious thoughts to those which cause us to feel grateful. Most of us walk around poorly tuned, so all that our receivers pick up are the signals that cause us discomfort, that help us to notice what is wrong or what needs fixing, or what is lacking in our lives—"It's cold and rainy outside," "I don't have enough_____," "I have to do everything around here." We are so absorbed in this kind of thinking that we often walk right past gifts that are practically laid at our feet!

I wonder how many gifts you may have already bypassed receiving today? I am often amazed when I catch myself saying "no" to a kind offer or even feeling uncomfortable when someone goes out of their way for me. I remember once as we were leaving a hotel in a drizzling rain, my husband offered to walk to the car and bring it to the door for me. At first I turned him down by telling him that I wasn't worried about getting a little bit wet, until I realized that he was showing me how much he cared for me. This wonderful man was expressing his love for me, and I was about to reject his gift! My tuner was turned to the OFF position. This small event was a major epiphany for me that showed me that I needed to refocus my point of view and learn the meaning of receiving gracefully, and the art of doing so.

Often, but not always, receiving involves asking. Asking is opening the door and inviting the gift. Asking is one way to turn on our receiver. Even if the request is declined, we have received something. We have received a reply that in our most grace-filled moments we can acknowledge and appreciate. Many times, however, we do not ask for what we are wanting and find ourselves resenting not having what we desire. Often we do not ask because we may be afraid of looking needy, of being a burden, of feeling unworthy, or of bothering someone. This list can go on and on. The truth is, when we do not ask we are blocking channels to manifesting and to receiving.

The best and most graceful way of asking is politely and directly. You will likely be very pleasantly surprised at how willing and even eager others are to being helpful when they know exactly what you want, when you want it, and how you want it, when you just put aside your fears and ask. Then receiving gracefully is a no-brainer! A heartfelt thank you is all that is necessary.

The same is true with any kind of obvious gift of time, material goods, attention, compliments, or love. How often is a gift met with some form of deprecation? "Oh, that wasn't necessary," "This is too much," "You really shouldn't have." These kinds of responses energetically block the good feelings in the moment, when all we really want is to feel closer and more connected. Often the best and most graceful response is a simple thank you. The expression of gratitude tunes us in to more signals that gifts are coming our way.

Less obvious in the world of grace are the opportunities to receive that come disguised. When Vanessa asked me to contribute a chapter to the writing of this book, my immediate response was no. I rationalized that I was too busy with other projects, and that writing has not been my focus lately. She then came back to me a few weeks later with another offer, and I thought about it some more, and no ideas came to me for a topic. Several weeks later as this book was beginning to come together for Vanessa, she found that she was one chapter shy of the right number and she again came to me, offering me the opportunity one last time. I told her I would sleep on it, which is exactly what I did.

That night I went to bed asking for an answer about the book and a topic. I was awakened from my sleep by what felt like a smack on the back of my head by an angel wing and a voice that said, "Just say thank you." So here I am receiving this wonderful gift from Vanessa.

Since this realization, I have twice given myself the twenty-four hour assignment to say yes to every offering that comes my way. Each of those days has proven to be very powerful for me. Never before was I able to so clearly see how much abundance flows into my life on a daily basis. Just today, I have said yes to people offering to serve me coffee, drive me to the airport, give me their chair, bring me a blanket for my nap, cook for me . . . for a few examples.

When our tuners are switched on and dialed in to the frequency of receiving we are able to perceive all of the blessings that are coming our way. Being fully present to see the blessings, saying yes to them, and expressing heartfelt gratitude are the keys to receiving gracefully.

Dear Universe: Yes, please, and thank you!

Dr. Robin Kirby is a Heart Centered Therapist in Atlanta, Georgia who works with individuals, couples, and families to overcome the obstacles to living happy and joyful lives.
www.lovingimpact.com

Day 18

Today, I choose a thought of
Persistence

by Christian Belz

Stephen was fat. He panted, bending over to tie his shoes. His pants grew tighter around his waist. Over the last year, he had gained twenty pounds on top of his already excessive weight. He tried repeatedly to diet, exercise, and lose weight. He had done it before. But each time he started over he fell off his plan, and in frustration he stuffed his face with nachos, pizzas, and French fries—with chili and cheese. Soon his expanding belly caused his pants zipper to break. The tugging at his shirt buttons was simply embarrassing. But it wasn't until his paunch caused him trouble sleeping that he changed his plan of attack.

Lying in bed one night, he moved his fat gut around to get comfortable. He breathed hard, and, for the first time, wondered if his weight might cause him to die. He panicked. What if he died and left his college-age kids without a father? And what about the grandkids? Surely his sons would soon wed and start having children. No, no, no! This was unacceptable!

The next morning, he wrote down reasons to lose weight and get fit. He started with "be around for the kids," and "fit and healthy for the grandchildren," and added other things he would do with newfound fitness. With a fresh perspective, he began again. He read his list of reasons often, sometimes several times a day, and over the next seven months he lost 56 pounds and started running 10K races.

Persistence means to move steadfastly in the direction of our goals, no matter what delays, setbacks, and disappointments we encounter. After Stephen began again, things weren't perfect. He had bad food days. There were days he woke up late and skipped exercise. He experienced temptation—and indulgence—at holidays. But he repeatedly referred to his list of goals, recharged his vision, and recommitted to succeeding.

Continually, our challenge is to find the drive to push forward in the face of adversity. While obstacles may strike from outside ourselves—withdrawal of support from friends, financial problems, car trouble—the main problem thwarting our progress frequently lies within our own thoughts and feelings.

Try this exercise. Think of your first love, the dizzy moment you initially felt your heightened emotions. Reflect on the hours you shared together. What feelings present themselves today, right now, at your reflection of those memories? Perhaps love or joy, maybe regret or sadness. Do you feel energized or depleted, more motivated to do something right now, or less motivated?

Do you see how our emotions can be harnessed to strengthen our perseverance, or if left unchanneled, how they may undermine it?

Perhaps there are feelings we avoid. If we don't like to feel stupid, we tend to avoid taking risks which might result in having that experience. But when we stay in our comfort zones, we miss a lot. Much of the "good stuff" in this life waits for us on the other side of the risk of feeling embarrassed, stupid, or silly. As we maintain our commitment to our goals, the road may put us up against those very emotions. Do we take the risk and move forward, or do we stay safe? What do we give up by staying in our comfort zones?

We must challenge ourselves to use emotions as blessings which work in our favor. The logical thoughts, the intellectual arguments, may or may not buttress our resolution. But when we tune in to what drives us—like Stephen did—those emotions act to invigorate us and strengthen our march forward. A factual argument like "I need a job so I can pay bills" may not energize us. We need to seek the why in our goals: what important things are at stake? What threatens to make our blood boil or bring our hearts to dance? An emotional incentive, such as "I need to find a job to pay for my mom's surgery" will drive us to take action.

Do you see how finding the right reasons will bring emotions to the forefront, emotions which will motivate us to break through our roadblocks?

Sometimes our resolve is aided by stepping back and taking the long view of the path we're on. This allows us to look beyond the events of this week, past the ups, the downs, the delays, setbacks, and disappointments. Our lives are a graph of mountains and valleys, a seismic chart of localized tremors. If we take in the overall picture, the long view, we see the direction of our progress. Is it leading upward? Have we have made strides toward our goals? Do we see how far we've come?

There will be downs. Accept them and learn what needs improvement. During the course of his several-month journey, Stephen came to realize that certain foods drove him over the binge cliff. He also discovered that he was less likely to have a problem when eating with friends or co-workers. Consequently, he adjusted his plan by deciding to eat those foods only when dining with others.

Celebrate the ups as they arise. Accept them. Learn what methods succeeded and build upon them. Incorporate what works, drop what doesn't. Remember your emotional arguments, those gifts with the capacity to move you. Aim high, keep your eye on the target, and remind yourself of your purpose daily.

Right now, consider your goal. Write down your list of emotional reasons for succeeding. Read your list several times today. With persistence, you, too, can move beyond your obstacles and reach your goals. You will be rewarded with the emotional charge that comes with accomplishment.

Our stories can be glorious, no matter how low the lows have been, no matter what we've been through, no matter if we've given up, or how often we've failed—for we haven't failed, not really, if we pull ourselves up one more time, refocus on what moves us, and try again.

Christian Belz has been a practicing architect in Metro Detroit for 28 years. He won the Grand Prize in Aquarius Press's 2011 Bright Harvest Prize and his short stories have been published in the Journal of Microliterature, Over My Dead Body, The Storyteller Magazine, and Writers' Journal.

Today, I choose a thought of

Courage

by Monserrat del Carmen Pineda

Angelic guidance has always played a key role in my life. Sadly, it took a long time for me to openly acknowledge and embrace this divine mentorship in its many forms. A Divinity whose gentle guidance and communion brought protection numerous times throughout my life, and yet I struggled, fearful and unable to step over the imaginary quicksand I thought I would drown in if I ever told anyone other than family or friends.

Several years crumbled by due to my unwillingness to speak my truth about what I had seen, felt, and known at the core of my very being during my communion with the Divine. I felt bad about my inability to share with others the details of my frequent mystical and synchronous experiences, but I was worried about what consequences it would bring. I had no desire to be mocked by the media, business associates, or anyone else for that matter. I had seen what other braver souls had endured when their stories came out, and the reaction was often unfortunate.

Being of sound mind would not be enough to dissuade skeptics from reacting, and in my mind, being unable to provide physical evidence for any of my experiences created apprehension at the thought of coming forward. The uncertainty of sharing any details often left me agonizing about what judgment would be hurled upon me, whether in the corporate world or in my own community. Instead, I continued to hide, suffering by silence.

The self-imposed censorship over time rendered my body out of alignment. I was always feeling stressed, constantly tired, and enraged. Keeping quiet had left me feeling dejected and stuck, yet I was too afraid to speak my truth.

This is why I offer you the gift of *COURAGE*, a word so instrumental in my own healing process. I offer it to you with Grace, to guide, heal, and prompt anyone else feeling stuck and afraid to make changes in life.

The fear of something is an opportunity to transcend. Finding *courage* was an exhausting process, and it was hidden under layers of toxic beliefs and fear. To understand what was holding me back took a lot of reflection; seeking a new chapter in life, I set out to discover what was keeping me stuck. In the end, it was all so simple. The discovery process brought me back into alignment and I finally understood the reason for my own stagnation.

As we strive to move forward in our lives, take notice of what is keeping you chained. Is it a thought, a belief, a memory? So often we humans forget our true divine identities and connection to spirit as we live in our human form on earth. We come in as divine spirits here to experience physical life, to learn something, and to do something before we return.

We all have good intentions to make the most of our experiences on earth, yet so often we become afraid of life in the process. Until the moment we courageously transcend fear, we will continue to struggle. It may be struggles with careers, issues in relationships, or challenges in our health. The manifestation is the same—a life lived out of alignment, stuck, hurting and yearning for more, but too paralyzed by fear to make a change.

Creating barriers, imposing limitations on yourself, and being fearful sets you up to being out of alignment. This resistance and fear to change is a dense energy which keeps life unbalanced, not in harmony. The cycle of struggle continues until its source is identified, brought forward, and released.

It takes *courage* to peel back the layers and heal the wounds caused by these dense energies. To awaken to my true potential I opted to speak, trusting Spirit openly on an atomic level. To battle the shadows, I had to be able to connect openly to the light. It eased my process for change because where there is light, there is no darkness. It takes *courage* to live life connected and spiritually opened, and that is what keeps me centered and balanced.

We can profoundly change our lives by the thoughts and actions we choose. By being in harmony and aligned with who we are spiritually, along with what we want to experience and offer the world, we can live life in resonance while we are in this human form.

Shifting one's resonance is a deeply personal process of intense and deep reflection. It takes *courage* to shift. Be open during your healing discovery process. Shifting your perception about what is or isn't happening is key. You may think an issue is happening to you; instead, it may be happening for you.

Know that you are receiving angelic guidance at all times and you simply need to pay attention. When you step out of your bondage to fear and step into your truth, know that you will be supported and blessed on a grander scale.

Whether you choose meditation, prayer, self-reflection, or silence as your gateway to enlightenment, know that all knowledge you seek will unfold in accordance to your own divine plan, purpose, and in perfect time. You will be supported and aligned and more in sync. Be courageous, be bold, and trust that this is so.

When you are being who you are meant to be and doing what you are meant to do, life will flow easily, magnified with Grace. When we unfold from the inside, we create a ripple or wave that affects and shifts the vibration we emanate. This not only heals our wounds from the inside, it amplifies affecting others exponentially.

I invite you to step into your truth, and let the discovery of *courage* be the gift you receive today.

I wish to extend my gratitude to Vanessa Lowry and all contributing authors in this book for bringing a beacon of hope and wisdom for all aligned to hear its message.

Monserrat del Carmen is a Technical Talent Scout and Intuitive Consultant for VIPs and High Profile Entrepreneurs. She is recognized as a Multi-Dimensional Healer, Teacher, and Leader in new thought paradigms. Monserrat is a gifted intuitive with documented Technical Remote Viewing skills, aligned and mentored by the Divine Angelic Realm.
www.monserratdelcarmen.com

Day 20

Today, I choose a thought of
Self-Love

by Nanette Littlestone

Do you love yourself? If you answered yes, how much? Just a little? Or a lot? Do you love yourself only when you feel good or even when you feel bad? What about when you fail a test, or don't get a raise, or can't fit into the new clothes you bought? What if you could love yourself, really love yourself, all the time?

The word "love" has over twenty definitions, ranging from the act of love to doing something gratuitously. You can love your husband, your cat, and your country. You can love ice cream, the way light shines through the curtains, and how the sun makes you feel warm and drowsy. But how do you love yourself?

Self-love: love of yourself and the awareness of who you truly are.

The term "self-love" means the love of oneself, the instinct or desire to promote one's own well-being. True self-love is not narcissistic or self-indulgent. It is an awareness of your inner power. A knowledge of who you really are. Without self-love, the soul can't flourish. Marianne Williamson speaks about the soul in these brilliant words: "Our deepest fear is not that we are inadequate. Our deepest fear is that we are powerful beyond measure. It is our light, not our darkness that most frightens us." Are you hiding your light? Does your soul long to shine? Have you nurtured your childhood dreams?

Dreams are tied to your inner gifts. If you love nature, you might be a doctor, herbalist, or zoologist. If you love finger paints, you could be an artist, fashion consultant, or graphic designer. Those stirrings inside you are meant to point your way. Self-love acknowledges who you are and what you like. By cultivating your gifts, you show your true passions to the world. Your light illuminates the way for others and allows them to shine as well. My love of words led me to reading, then writing, then editing, and eventually to a marriage of all three—being a writing coach.

So how do you start loving yourself? Here are five ways to begin the journey.

1. *Address self-sabotage.* Does the little voice in your head say you're not good enough, not smart enough, not pretty enough, or you don't have enough experience? Those negative thoughts and beliefs stem from past experience. Maybe you didn't date as soon as other boys and girls in your class. Or you were picked last for the softball team. Or you just weren't good at math. These beliefs are lodged in your unconscious. Before you can practice self-love you need to let them go. You can heal these thoughts through a myriad of techniques like hypnotherapy, coaching, EFT (Emotional Freedom Technique, otherwise known as tapping), and the Sedona Method, to name a few. Find a process that resonates with you and stick with it. By changing your beliefs, you allow the real you to emerge.

I love myself just the way I am.

2. *Use affirmations.* Affirmations are positive statements of something you want in your life. They help pave the way for the subconscious mind. By using affirmations, you train your mind to develop new ways of thinking. If you're trying to lose weight, you could say, "I am at

the perfect weight for my body." If you're trying to attract more clients, you could state, "I easily attract the perfect clients for my business." Here are some self-love affirmations to get you started.

I love myself just the way I am.

I appreciate who I am right now.

I let go of my fears and go forward with confidence.

3. *Appreciate yourself.* Look in the mirror. Really look in the mirror. Do you like what you see? When was the last time you told yourself how beautiful or handsome you are? Do it now. Maybe you're not crazy about your wrinkles or your gray hair. Maybe you wish you were taller or shorter. Start with what you do like and really love that part of you. The more you do this, the more you'll be able to incorporate parts of you that you didn't like before. And when you truly love yourself, others will too.

4. *Be creative.* What do you love to do? Do you love to play with color? Are you amazed by the power of words? Do you go crazy over fabric or glass or stone? Have you always wanted to make something with your hands? Give yourself permission to follow that voice inside your head, the one that's saying "can I, can I?" Play. Explore. Discover. Embracing your passions is a sure way to love yourself. You might even find a new career. If you're not sure what you love, take the Passion Test at www.thepassiontest.com.

Please forgive me.

5. *Practice forgiveness.* Have you ever criticized yourself for a mistake you made? Or beat yourself up because you didn't do something well? Criticizing yourself or comparing yourself to others only hurts you. Sometimes

it's hard to remember you're not perfect. Holding on to that resentment can damage your health. Forgiveness is a way to heal and move forward with peace and love. The Hawaiians have a beautiful forgiveness prayer called Ho'oponopono. It's just four simple lines.

I'm sorry

Please forgive me

I love you

Thank you

Saying these words, with feeling, can unlock those hurts and restore your self-love.

These five methods are just some of the ways to practice self-love and engage in loving thoughts. The more you love yourself, the more you step into your power. Pierre Teilhard de Chardin said, "We are not human beings having a spiritual experience. We are spiritual beings having a human experience." Experience the love that is rightfully yours. Let your light shine. Be the amazing person you can be.

Begin your day with *"Today, I choose a thought of self-love."*

Nanette Littlestone is a writing coach, editor, author, and speaker. She combines nearly 20 years of expertise with both fiction and nonfiction to help inspirational authors write with clarity and passion. **www.wordsofpassion.com**

Day 21

Today, I choose a thought of
Acceptance

by Sharon S. Smith

Today, I choose the thought of acceptance. For with this choice I gain passage to a haven where calm and peace await in the knowingness that I am not alone. On the same journey together, we all march toward a common destiny. The acceptance of this thought lifts my spirit, buoys my hope, and silences my fear. I choose acceptance with the intention to share all its trappings with others as I celebrate this new day.

If you have not explored this incredible place or visited it lately, I invite you to walk along with me. Chart your own course to acceptance where the treasures of hope, fearlessness, and renewed spirit lie. My journey started in a most unpredictable way, unaided by books, CDs, coaching, therapy, or a doctor's prescription. Rather, it began with a furry, fearless 10-pound dog. Meet Zoe. This beautiful creature bounded into my life a year after the passing of my beloved father. Not in touch with the true depth of my sorrow from this loss, I was ecstatic to have this adorable puppy and tend to her needs. Something to dote on; she should be a fun distraction.

As with anything electrical, she should have come with a bold warning tag. "INSTRUCTIONS: This dog will steal your heart. Buckle up! You're in for a bumpy ride!" Yet, while I focused on navigating along the "puppyhood on our way to becoming a grown up girl" road, Zoe was heading down a very different road. With ease, she breezed through the lessons every growing puppy must learn. Unaware, my own lesson had begun.

She seemed to be showing me something that at first glance was simply delightful entertainment, greeting each new day with unbridled enthusiasm. Wag. Wag. Run in circles. And then, of course, more wags! I'd laugh out loud and say, "Zoe, we have a new day everyday, little one! We'll get to do this all over again tomorrow." Note to self: "A puppy living in the moment is your teacher. We are given the animal we need." She fascinated me. She glided through all of her todays accepting everything about her life, everything that came her way, delighted to be at my side. She exuded joy. Each day she effortlessly dished up a super-sized serving of her buoyant spirit, her gift to anyone who was willing to accept it, to those willing to see it. And I began accepting because I was willing to see. Much more than a distraction, with her as my guide, my lesson was taking shape. I kidded friends and family that she had become my "dog"ther, the daughter I never had and always wanted. I became deeply grateful to have her, and tearfully shared this with a trusted few—those I was confident could be bribed if they tried to commit "the lady who was crazy about a silly little dog."

And then the bumpy ride began. Zoe had a lump. This discovery was crushing, and I struggled to catch my breath. With a protocol in hand, I prayed it was the Cure for My Canine; but my heart sank as we left the vet's office. Fear set in and I buckled up for dear life clutching Zoe in my arms. Alone with her she would quietly, calmly gaze at me with soft dark eyes while I stroked her, and I would often whisper, "Little Zoe, you have to get rid of the lump. Mommy needs you to be well." After two weeks of worry, little sleep, and raw despair, I lay on the couch, cuddling her. And when tears once again rolled down my face from the anguish of possibly losing her (We just got started, little Zoe!), something incredible happened. Calmness took hold allowing these comforting words to appear. "You will have her for as long as you are to have her." Simple. Accepting. No fear. This purity is the place I now call acceptance.

My spirit was lifted; what followed next was long awaited. Finally, after 5 years, acceptance of my father's death. Like a dutiful student under the watch of my teacher, I looked into her soft eyes and recited, "I had him as long as I was to have him." Thank you, little Zoe, for leading me here.

I've created a mental image. A grand doorway with the letters "ACCEPTANCE" above it acts as a street address, ensuring I find my way back. This door is always ajar, accessible; a warm light peeks through reminding me what lies inside. My frequent travels here will surely, in time, smooth the stones underfoot along my way. So, too, let your path here be one well worn. Set your GPS to destination acceptance where we learn much about loving others and ourselves. The lessons of what is our business, what is not, and what is His are easier learned here. Here we can let go, and do so without fear. For Zoe (which I have since learned is Greek for LIFE), for my father, for today's challenges, I visit this place where the "bumps" are cured and there is no need to buckle up.

Construct your own place such as this. Enlist whomever, whatever you can to get you there. Live each day with an accepting heart where little room remains for judgment and meddling. Grace the world and treat others with acceptance. I start each day with acceptance. I accept friend's idiosyncrasies knowing this makes me a better me. Without doubt or question, I accept the unconditional love of my spouse. I choose acceptance in the face of family differences as an ever-loving child, a kind sibling. And for each of you, friends or strangers united by our common destiny, I offer you my story of acceptance. For I am free to be my best self because I am now unbuckled, without fear. *Today, I choose a thought of acceptance.*

 Sharon S. Smith is passionate about wellness and is owner of Thrive Nutrition. She is also a community advocate, raising funds for pet life saving gear through her project, Oxygen Fur Pets.
www.thrivenutrition.net
www.facebook.com/OxygenFurPets

A person who has good thoughts can never be ugly. You can have a wonky nose, and a crooked mouth, and a double chin, and sticky-out teeth, but if you have good thoughts, they will shine out of your face like sunbeams and you will always look **lovely.** ~ Roald Dahl

Today, I choose a thought of
Resilience

by Sandy Weaver Carman

Do you ever wake up feeling like you can't make it through the day? Do you mentally tick off the many challenges you face and wonder if you'll be up to them all? Do you feel out of your depth, or even worse, like an imposter in your own life?

Growing up in a military family meant we moved a lot. Our address changed so often that I had bad dreams of not being able to find the right classroom, causing me to flunk out of school! That was how the stress of changing schools manifested in my childhood—being lost in my dreams, and in my waking hours, having a serious desire to do well in class so if I did actually get lost one day, it wouldn't be the end of my grades.

When I was 17, we moved from Northern California to Columbus, Georgia, and the difference in culture couldn't have been more stark. I remember going to school on the first day wearing a stylish skirt and matching top—an outfit that would have been perfect at my old school but that was ridiculed in this new one. Money was stolen from my handbag while the teacher was in the room, and no one ever got caught. Worst of all was the morning that I discovered this new school had segregated stairwells. The students were the ones who segregated them, and I found out about the unofficial rules by choosing the wrong set of stairs. I heard "White girl on our stairs!" just before a hand shoved me from behind. My books and purse went flying and I tumbled down the stairs after them, but thankfully the only thing seriously wounded was my pride. The guidance counselor told me to let it go and use the correct stairwell in the future.

I did not want to go back to that school.

For the first time in my life, I wanted to blend in. I wanted to fly under the radar until graduation, and then forget that awful school and awful chapter of my life and move on.

Perhaps you've had similar experiences—times when you were faced with something you dreaded on a daily basis. It could have been school, work, health, or worse yet, it could have been something going on in your own home. That "something" made you want to give up a part of yourself, which is what "blending in" is all about. When you "blend in," you hand someone else control of your soul, your creativity, and your life. You let them dictate your behavior, dress, words, and even thoughts. You give up.

Mom knew how tough that move was, but I'm not sure she ever knew how badly I wanted to crawl under a rock and hide for the rest of my senior year. She helped me adapt my wardrobe so it was more like what the rest of the kids wore to school. She gently reminded me not to leave my pay envelope from my after-school job in my purse when I went to school. And she made sure I understood that someone who harms another person does so because of a deficiency of humanity in their heart, not because of an abundance of melanin in their skin.

She kept me focused on creative pursuits outside of school—art classes at the museum, arrowhead and shark tooth hunting after a rainstorm, and treasure hunts in local antique shops, junk stores, and garage sales.

She saw my enthusiasm for school wane, but she made sure there was something to look forward to after school.

I don't know whether she did this by instinct or by plan, but either way, she understood that what I was suddenly lacking was resilience. And as an expression of that lack, I was letting school and the people there change me and control me.

Mom wasn't a religious woman, but she was spiritual. She had a bible highlighted with colored pencils, illuminating her favorite passages. One of them was from Corinthians, and it talked about thriving no matter what circumstance you found yourself in. Her version of that passage was "bloom where you are planted" and she found a little wooden gardening box, complete with tiny gardening tools, with those words stenciled on it.

She used that garage-sale find as a conversation starter. We talked about how many times we had moved before, how things sometimes worked out really well and sometimes not so well, how some places had surprised us with their beauty when we were expecting desolation, and how some dismayed us with their depressing, grey, rainy days for months on end. And we talked about how we had survived it all and thrived in spite of circumstances we didn't choose.

"Bloom where you are planted" became the words I thought when I awoke each weekday. "Bloom where you are planted" became the shield I used when I entered school each morning. "Bloom where you are planted" became the way my resilience returned, slowly but surely.

I survived my senior year, even earning top honors. I was probably slightly more excited to graduate than most seniors are, and over the years I have put the negative aspects of that time out of my mind.

When Mom passed away, Dad made sure that I got the little set of garden tools. They continue to inspire me to this day, and they make me smile every time I look at them.

Today, I choose a thought of resilience because resilience makes every challenge manageable, every obstacle surmountable, and every test passable.

Today, I choose a thought of resilience, and I thank Mom for guiding my thoughts with those little tools.

Sandy Weaver Carman partners with writers, speakers, trainers, and coaches, taking work they've already done and turning it into a revenue river. She is CEO of Voicework on Demand, Inc., an audio production company specializing in audio books and products. **www.voiceworkondemand.com**

Today, I choose a thought of
Being Willing

by Vanessa Lowry

Have you ever needed a step stool? Often in my life journey, a new want is out of my immediate reach. *Being willing* is the tool to help me get what I want.

When I, who had never been athletic, started training in martial arts in my mid-thirties, it was willingness that kept me going to achieve a second-degree black belt in karate. Being willing to be a beginner. Being willing to be sore . . . every day for about a year. Being willing to often be the oldest person in the class. Being willing to continually make small adjustments when I didn't do a punch or a kick correctly the first few hundred times.

Being willing is the step to move to the next level.

A few months ago, my friend Patrice died. Her memorial service was a celebration of her life. People who loved Patrice shared the multitude of ways she had helped people, how she made them laugh, and how she lived her life with enthusiasm.

Talking with my husband Ben a few days later, I said that when I died, I wanted people to say, "Vanessa lived a creative life, she loved people and they knew it." Then I continued, "I would also like for them to say 'and she was fearless.' But, that's never going to happen." We laughed about it.

93

The next day Ben said, "I think you should start believing that you ARE fearless. You might be surprised at what happens if you declare that." I couldn't go directly to "I am fearless," but I started saying, "I am willing to act as if I am fearless." This was a slight shift, but seemed more attainable to me.

Within a week, one of my clients said to me, "That's easy for you—you're fearless!" What! Me, fearless? I had to laugh. The Universe had quickly responded to my desire to be fearless with evidence that someone else already saw me that way. Feeling fearless is within my grasp some days and almost nonexistent on others. The reminder to be willing is a step stool on days I need a little assistance.

Being willing gives you a broader perspective.

I was introduced to the work of Byron Katie as my business, Profits in Progress, was closing nearly five years ago. Katie teaches a method of observing an upsetting or angry thought, then turning your thought around to see if the opposite is equally true. After stating alternate versions of the thought, you list all the reasons that these alternate realities could equally be true. You choose which of these "truths" leave you feeling more hopeful and more engaged in life.

With my business's lack of success—which I believed at that time to be a personal failure—I really needed a new perspective to see myself differently. So, I started with the shame-filled statement, "I am a failure." I made supporting statements like, "I lost a great deal of money and incurred enormous debt." "I am a disappointment to my family and friends." "No one will trust me enough to hire me."

Using the practice of being willing, I moved to "My business failed, but 'I' am not a failure." With supporting statements, "I am willing to believe that the people I met through this failed business journey will contribute to my future success." "I am willing to learn from this experience to see myself and others with more compassion."

"I am willing to learn from innovators like Walt Disney and Steve Jobs who experienced failures, reinvented their lives, and made enormous contributions to the world." "I am willing to identify what success means for me instead of measuring my success by the standards of others."

Being willing has renewed my artistic expression.

My current art medium is doodling. As I fill the page with colorful doodles, I remind myself to be willing to add a new shape or a different color. I can feel my perfectionist thoughts saying I might mess it up. My inner artist reminds me that this is just a doodle. I can do another one if this one is ruined. It's an experiment.

As I continue to add to the page, sometimes in short drawing sessions over several days, I always come to a point when I like the doodle again.

It reminds me that life is an experiment. Just like my doodle, if I get to a point where it isn't looking particularly good, I just keep going. Being willing to add new combinations of shapes and colors—and in life new knowledge, people, and experiences—the art, and my life, eventually come to a cohesive beauty.

Being willing creates opportunities to express creativity and follow your dream.

I remember watching a lecture series by Bruce Wilkinson expanding on his bestselling book *The Dream Giver*. What I remember from the lecture was, "What if the reason there are unmet needs in the world is because YOU aren't fulfilling your dream?"

The quote is my paraphrase of Dr. Wilkinson's comment, but it stuck with me. Even when I'm feeling like I don't know enough or don't have the resources to move forward, this comes to mind. It helps me be willing to take a next step, realizing my progress may help someone else.

The last few lines of a popular quote by Marianne Williamson says, "As we are liberated from our own fear, our presence automatically liberates others."

As I have been willing to put my stories, doodles, and inspirations on paper, I've found others are inspired to their own creative expression. Even in this collaborative book project, one of the co-authors said, "You have jumpstarted me back onto my other writing project."

Today, I choose a thought of being willing. I hope you will too.

Vanessa Lowry is a marketing consultant, graphic designer, author, radio host, and speaker. She leverages nearly 30 years of design and marketing expertise to support book authors who are self-publishing. **www.connect4leverage.com**

Day 24

Today, I choose a thought of

Progress

by Traci Long

We've all done it. Suffered in silence when we know we will feel much better if we picked up the phone and said three little words. I need help.

As women, we learn at an early age how to nurture and care for others, yet learning how to ask for help ourselves gets left out of the life curriculum somehow. When we are old enough to really understand the underlying message flight attendants are giving us as they tell us to put our own oxygen mask on first . . . it's too late. The guilt has set in. I can't ask for help. What would people think? Here's a little secret most people don't reveal. They like it when you ask for help. That's right. It makes them feel useful. Seriously, reflect for a moment on how you feel when someone asks you for help. I morph into Super Woman mode. On steriods. I can leap over piles of my undone laundry in a single second to help you when you are in a bind. You are a stranger and need assistance finding your way? Not a problem, I'll take you there as long as you don't figure out I'm lost too.

Ego, as defined by Webster, is "the self especially as contrasted with another self or the world." There are a lot of acronyms for EGO. Edging God Out or Everybody's Got One. Eyes Glazed Over may even apply here. The Ego causes us to do some very strange and often destructive things in the name of self-preservation. Life altering choices are made. Feelings are denied. Credit cards are maxed out. All in the name of putting pride before progress. It seems easier to just put that pair of "fabulous" shoes on your credit card instead of admitting to your girlfriend you can't afford them. All the while you are thinking "I hope they have a lenient return policy. I am so bringing these back tomorrow when she is not shopping with me!" How much better would you feel about yourself and your decisions if you made them from a place of core transparency as opposed to the filtered lens of pride?

Pride can creep in at the most inconvenient times. It can be the number one offender in keeping us stuck. We buy into the belief if people really knew how we felt, we would be ostracized from life as we know it. We sentence ourselves to a life of being forever alone with our own thoughts and the bag of orange-powdered Cheetos we'd go to our deathbed denying we ever bought, much less ate. It is the ultimate paradox. Pride keeps us from reaching out for fear we will end up being rejected and alone. We choose not to reach out, and we are essentially rejecting others and end up alone. A self-fulfilled prophecy in the highest degree.

Original Artwork by Cathie Parmelee
St. Simons Island, Georgia

I've experienced this myself in life and in business. I've watched hundreds of moms—entrepreneurs and close friends—repeat this cycle over and over again. They need help. They hit a wall with the kids but don't want to inconvenience anyone. They are overwhelmed in business and need a break but are fearful no one can run it like they run it. They are struggling with the emotional shrapnel from the relationship bomb that went off but they know their girlfriends didn't like him anyway. So they suffer in silence wondering how to fix it, heal it, or just simply get a reprieve from it.

Progress usually requires change. Pride usually keeps us from being willing to change. The easiest way to see progress from change is to not change all at once. Solid progress reflected from forward movement starts with small steps. Firstly, begin by noticing when your EGO is starting to inhibit your ability to make positive strides in the right direction. Become aware of the tape playing in your head that says, "I got this" or "Don't bother them, they are busy." Change the tape. The moment you first hear the voice driving you to alienate or alleviate the need to reach out is the time to hit the pause button. Rewind and Rephrase. Try a new thought. One with more kindness and honesty. One that gives you permission to do something differently.

Doing something differently is the key to successful change. But it's easier said than done in most cases. If I want to see long-term effective change I start with the easier tasks first and build up to the bigger changes. Make simple changes first. Start with calling three friends a day to ask how they are doing and speak honestly with them about how you are feeling and the struggles you may be facing in the moment. Learning to get honest with yourself and others about the little things will make the big life challenges much easier to reveal when they occur.

Secondly, get very clear about what it is that you need and learn how to ask for it. Try this out by paying attention to how you order your food in a restaurant. If you want the dressing on the side and prefer to have your chicken grilled rather than fried, ask for it. If your food arrives with fried chicken drenched in ranch dressing, politely explain it is not what you ordered and send it back. You will get the salad you wanted, but the real sustenance will come in being empowered by asking for what you needed and getting it.

Lastly, press forward. Putting aside your pride to do things differently does not come wrapped in a perfect package. You will stumble. It will be uncomfortable and may even feel like you are an alien in your own skin. But press forward. Keep the pride to a minimum and the progress will open a world of possibilities.

Traci Long is a consultant/speaker/strategist whose clients include Microsoft, The Applegate Group, and various global women entrepreneur organizations. Contact her at: tel@tracilong.com. **www.tracilong.com**

Day 25

Today, I choose a thought of

Letting Go

by Kyle Young

Okay, I admit it. I like to be in control. To have everything I need right at my fingertips. To be sure I have a plan B, and maybe even C, prepared for all eventualities. I imagine it all started when my little brother was born. From the beginning, I was his protector, defender, and friend. Then brothers two and three came along, so you can imagine the role I took on. Big Sister, substitute mom, keeper of the peace. In charge? No problem. I was praised by parents and teachers alike for being so "responsible."

Not a bad thing, in and of itself. It's good to be responsible. To meet your obligations and keep your promises. To be someone others know they can depend on. To live that "If it's to be, it's up to me!" attitude. But there is a downside to carrying all that responsibility. When you're so busy planning and hanging on to things for every possibility, it really doesn't leave much room for . . . well, anything other than what's on YOUR radar. No room for surprise. Synchronicity. Serendipity. For new things and unexpected people and circumstances to come into your life.

It's like having a closet full of clothes with nothing you want to wear! Where's the room for the season's latest trend if your closet is already bursting at the seams with past purchases? Why buy the season's first peaches if you haven't yet eaten the ones you still have in your freezer from last summer? My personal downfall? Books! I already have full shelves, but that doesn't stop me from buying the latest one that catches my interest. However, it does create piles that threaten to topple over as they grow higher and higher. Accumulating, but never letting go. Always adding to, but never subtracting from. Sigh.

Is it just me? I doubt it. But it's hard, isn't it? Knowing when to hold on and when to let go. What is too much or too many? What is enough? For me it all comes down to one thing . . . trust. When I can trust my needs will be met, I can let go. When I trust I have all that I need, I can release what no longer serves me. When I trust that whatever I do will be the right thing for me, I can give up control. And really, who do I think I am, anyway? Ultimately, all I'm really in charge of is how I respond. As the saying goes, I can be less responsible, when I am response-able.

Wow! That's pretty freeing when you think about it. So how does it play out in your life? When do you hold on? And when do you let go? How do you know? For me, it works something like this. If it holds a memory for me, I usually hang on to it. No, I don't "need" my mother's good china, but I remember eating on it every birthday and holiday growing up, so it stays. It's packed safely away to be taken out, used, and treasured when I want to feel her close to me.

The three black skirts I have hanging in my closet? Not so much. In fact, my closet (which is not all that large) is a constant source of decision angst for me. Keep? Give away? Don't wear it. Might need it. What a struggle! Usually at the change of seasons, I set aside time to try on everything I haven't worn recently. I decide right then and there whether those clothes deserve a continued place on my hangers OR they should be set free to serve someone else's fashion needs. (I've done this now for so many seasons, they recognize me when I drive up at Goodwill!)

People and situations? Now those are decidedly more complex. Hard to "try on" but equally important when it comes to making space in your life. That neighbor who lives down the street? The one who seems to drain all life and energy out of you in every conversation? Maybe it's time to let her go. But the friend who energizes you with just a quick text? I'd say she deserves more time and space in your life. If Sunday night finds you dreading the thought of walking into work even one more time . . . well, I wouldn't quit my job, but I certainly would spend some time thinking about what I REALLY wanted to be doing. And then start taking some small steps in that direction.

Holding on. Letting go. I guess the best example I can offer is this. When my son was small, he was constantly outgrowing his clothes as all kids do. Purging the drawers, sharing hand-me-downs with those who might use them, and then restocking in his "new" size became a regular part of life. So why not with us? As human beings, we are always "growing" in one way or another. Why not embrace, enjoy, and practice letting go so that new people, things, and experiences have room to come into your life?

Why not start today?

As Founder and CEO of one of Atlanta's Top 50 Advertising Agencies, **Kyle Young** was responsible for developing an award-winning team of varied and creative personalities. Now you can find Kyle blogging at **www.Multi-TaskingWoman.com** and sharing **www.EffectiveIdeas.com** for business and life. She continues to fine-tune her sense of when to hold on . . . and when to let go.

All that we are is the result of what we have thought. The mind is everything. What we think, we become. ~ Buddha

Day 26

Today, I choose a thought of
Listening

by Jim Hogan

Even before we could talk, we listened. We had no choice in the matter. By listening, we learned how to communicate with others through both verbal and nonverbal language.

We are really never taught to listen, but we are told to listen. "Listen to your father" means to do as your father says. Boy, does this bring back memories. As a child, I was not really listening but mechanically obeying the commands. Just look at your kids when you say this and you see their eyes roll and you know that they are thinking, *Here we go again.* The same goes for most business environments and bosses too. You do as you are told. Can you think of a time during your education when you actually were taught to listen or practiced listening skills? Why is that?

There is so much power in listening yet we choose to continue to talk, talk, talk, and tell others what we think. Since few people actually listen, why do we keep spewing words that do not connect or resonate with the receiver?

Seek first to understand, and then be understood. This old adage has been suggested as an important sales tool by some of the foremost sales trainers but few professional salespeople follow the advice. They are listening for that first objection, then reacting to overcome that objection, then the next objection, and so on.

Yes, overcoming objections is a tried and true sales technique that actually works and will very likely close the deal, but will it help create or advance a relationship with your client? Will it create a lifelong customer whose value increases exponentially?

If you really want to be a better listener, to listen with intent, then try to follow advice that has been handed down for ages. Always maintain eye contact and show agreement or acknowledgement through slight nods of the head. Please let the person talking finish their thought and don't interrupt. You are allowed to disagree, but do not interrupt or finish their sentence for them.

Be conscious of your nonverbal messages and make sure that you're congruent with the words you choose and the interest you show during your conversation. When it is your turn to speak, try to paraphrase their point in reply and if you disagree, remain respectful.

Talk less and listen more. You might have heard the saying: "You have two ears and one mouth, so use them in direct proportion." People will find you much more interesting if you follow this advice.

Social media has changed the way we communicate and the expectations associated with these communications. You can learn a lot about a person through today's social media and that is a good thing. It can be overwhelming, but the opportunities to expand your network are amazing. Take advantage of these tools and engage in conversations; listen and learn why people do what they do. It will be much easier to adapt your message once you know who they are, what they do, and why they do it.

Listening can keep you out of hot water during a disagreement or heated discussion. As an ice hockey official, it is my job to dispense justice and as you can imagine, there are numerous disagreements and differences of opinion. Listening can come in handy. It not only allows you to hear the other person's opinion, it gives you some extra time to carefully choose your words. My mentor, John Robinson, taught me: "Silence can never be misquoted." And this has served me well for 30 years on the ice.

Listening is a key to effective communication and if performed with intent, can reveal so much more information than the words themselves.

A wise old owl lived in an oak,
The more he saw, the less he spoke
The less he spoke, the more he heard.
Why can't we all be like that wise old bird?
~Author Unknown

Like the wise old owl, why don't you just choose to listen, really listen, just a little more today and every day?

Jim Hogan is a trainer with the Referral Institute who speaks to companies and groups on networking, referral marketing, and leveraging social media to reach their niche market and explode sales. **www.JimHogan.net**

If you don't like something, change it. If you can't change it, change your attitude. ~ Maya Angelou

Today, I choose a thought of
Feasting

by Jeanie Ward

Today, I choose a thought of feasting on the bountiful and beautiful "Banquet of Life" that I AM blessed to partake of every day. I AM mindful of every magnificent morsel offered in the endless array of abundance that nourishes my mind, body, heart, and soul. I AM enriched and energized as I engage Life with excitement and expectancy. Today, I walk my path with purpose and passion, in wonderment and awe of the divine and dazzling display of ALL that is, of the Substance that is generously and lovingly offered to me in this now moment. I AM reminded that as I consciously choose to serve my-Self, I AM, in service to others, aware of the Oneness that we share. I savor the sweetness of Spirit, delighted in my remembrance of why I AM here: "To Serve with Love."

One of the greatest gifts that we can offer another is what the Hindus call *seva*, which means service. Kahlil Gibran reminds us, "It is when you give of yourself that you truly give." Our divine nature is Love, flowing freely, fully, and fearlessly when we live from a grateful and generous heart. The art of giving and receiving is a delicate balance that requires commitment and can be consciously and lovingly developed over time.

In Western culture, the area of self-care and self-nurture in our lives, of "giving and receiving," is typically out of balance, albeit nonexistent, especially with women, as well as with some men. I believe many of us learned, early on, that "receiving" is selfish, thereby relegating "self-care" to the bottom of our "to-do" list, if it even makes it on the list at all. Today, *now*, is the *right and perfect* time to cultivate the art of self-care, remembering that *feasting* is elemental and essential in "serving" ourselves. Feast your eyes upon *nature* as an ever-present reminder of the law of giving and receiving— taking in (receiving) what is essential for Life to flow effortlessly while expressing (giving) elegantly in its natural form.

By choosing this book, you are demonstrating your innate desire to be nourished and to nourish others by giving yourself permission to feast from the table of truth, authenticity, joy, love, and freedom. During these 28 days, and for the rest of your life, I invite you to take time to be still, to enjoy everyday exquisite experiences that Life abundantly offers. Set your table of intention, mindfully preparing yourself to savor the succulence of Spirit, served 24/7. Divine Dining, at *Its* best! The menu is magnificent and every selection is prepared to perfection. No reservations are required. All you have to do is "arrive and allow" yourself to be filled with peace, grace, and loving kindness. Relax, renew, and *remember* that your divine birthright is joy, abundance, and wholeness.

Wholeness is borne out of freedom. The freedom to live authentically, uniquely, and divinely as you serves your best and highest good, simultaneously serving the good of All, elevating awareness that another choice is always at hand, in any given moment, *calling* you, again and again, to choose wisely and lovingly. *Feasting* is a conscious, nurturing choice, an intentional "practice" based in SELF-love, worthiness, and Oneness. Abundance and joy flow easily from the fountain of freedom, accompanying authenticity, repeatedly returning us to Source, every time, all the time, as we surrender to the divine flow, knowing that we have chosen well.

Each of us is responsible for the choices we make, and the outcome of those choices upon ourselves and others, individually and collectively. As spiritual beings inhabiting a human body, we are *called*, in every moment, to awaken to a greater understanding of who and what we are, why we are here, and to express our divine essence as unconditional love and compassion. I suspect that most of us were not taught to make conscious choices based in love, but more often based in fear, lack, and limitation. The thought of *feasting* on a "bountiful and beautiful banquet" may initially feel a bit uncomfortable, possibly even frightening. It's okay. What a perfect time to feast on your breath, trusting It to relax and reassure you that "all is well" regardless of the illusion that may have shown up at your feast, uninvited. Be gentle with yourself in moments of "uncomfortableness," perhaps when those uninvited "guest" thoughts appear or old beliefs beg to be fed. Give yourself permission to simply acknowledge them, releasing them through your breath while returning yourself to the *beauty of the feast*.

Old habits die hard, as do fear-based experiences, along with negative, unloving thoughts that have been stored in our cellular memories. What a blessing and gift to know that we can *feast* on the endless array of divine delicacies, always prepared with the right and perfect ingredients to satisfy any craving and desire of our mind, body, heart, and soul. *Feasting* vitalizes us, elevates our vibration, and is essential to healing and radiant well-being.

What will you have today? Possibly some *unlearning and remembering*, or perhaps *forgiveness and surrender* may offer you transcendent and transformational energies to enrich your feasting experience, satisfying your soul's craving for conscious communion with Source, sparking your body's return to its natural state of vitality and harmony. How about a cup of kindness, a bowl of blessings, a helping of humility, served with a side of serenity, to ease your mind and soothe your soul, infusing every cell of your fiber and "being" with the Infinite?

Remember, if you're not sure what you want, the Universal Chef is always preparing exactly what you need. All you need to do is ask, and it will be served per your request. Maybe today is your day to try something new, trusting that every bite is a blessing, every mouthful is magnificent, awakening you to a divine, delicious, and abundant experience of All That Is—All That You Are!

Savor the *"Beauty of the Feast!"* Bon Appetit!

In Love and Gratitude,

Jeanie Ward

Jeanie Ward, BA in Psychology, Inspirational Speaker, Author, Interfaith Minister, Spiritual Mentor, Women's Wellness Coach. Jeanie has been touching hearts and lives for over thirty years, inspiring people to reawaken to their own magic and magnificence, living fully, freely, and authentically. **www.jeanieward.com**

Day 28

Today, I choose a thought of

Endless Possibilities

by Laura McGill

As children we were taught that we could be anything we wish to be. Go anywhere we wished to go. Yet somewhere along the way many of us have forgotten this. Once a tiny little miracle with endless possibilities, we have grown and gone on to live the life of responsibility, mortgages, and bills. Living to work, not working to LIVE. Some of us have even had the gift of creating our own tiny miracles . . . our children. And what do we tell them? That they can be anything they wish to be and go anywhere they want to go. We truly believe this. So why have we forgotten this about ourselves? The best way to teach our children and to honour ourselves as God's children is to come to the realization that we still have these possibilities. This is what God, as our parent, wants for us.

Many of us have been stopped by fear in the past. Fear of failure, of what other people will think or say. One of the best ways and first steps in realizing your dreams is to walk past or even through those fears. Today go do something that terrifies you. Stand up in the middle of a shopping centre and read a love poem to the crowd. Dance to music on a busy sidewalk. Submit your manuscript that has been creating dust for months. Speak your truth. Scary . . . you bet. But when you do this you will be shifting your energy to a higher frequency. A frequency of trust, joy, and accomplishment. And guess what? The next frightening challenge you face, won't seem so bad. So many of us have stayed trapped in time by fear until God steps in and, with a push of love, forces us to move forward with our dreams. Let's move forward on our own now with God and our Angels walking beside us.

Nourish your body with healthful foods and drink. Eat organic. Fill your body with the rich colors of Mother Earth's natural fruits and vegetables. Let nature support you and fill you with the energy and vitality needed to live well. This is to me as much as it is you. Set the diet cola down and drink your fill of fresh, clear, cleansing water.

Read, read, and read some more. Expanding your mind will open your imagination and get that creative section in your brain turning. Take that journey to the center of the earth. Be swept away in the arms of a rugged cowboy. Lose yourself in the mystical patterns of the constellations.

Write. Write about your hopes and dreams. Where would you like to travel? What landmarks are crying out for you to see, touch, smell? Be descriptive. Are there fish nibbling your toes as you dip them into the salty, cool water of the ocean? Is the wind whipping through your hair as you stand on a cliff in the highlands of Scotland? Visualization is a huge part of creating and manifesting your dreams.

Paint, sketch, sculpt, collage, create from your soul. Even if you've never done any of these before. Dig out your crayola and go for it! Use as much texture, color and depth as you can. Stick figure yourself onto the moon and place it on your fridge as a reminder and expansion of where you are going.

Spend time alone. Listen to music, meditate, or in my case, put your baby down for a nap and take a long hot bath. Moments alone help center and ground you. It is in these moments when you can place life aside and find yourself.

Help others realize their possibilities. Volunteer at Big Brothers and Big Sisters. Take a child to the library, on an adventure hike, to a movie. Walk dogs at the animal shelter and pet the cats. Donate clothing and food. Most importantly, share your love, your smile, your kindness, yourself!

Be grateful for the possibilities that have been given to you in your life thus far. Nothing opens your life more than gratitude. Thank you, God, for all I have. Thank you, God, for who I am! Amen.

Pray and pray often. God and the Angels are always here to help. Let's invite them into our lives daily and let them assist us in finding our way.

Let's love ourselves as we love our children. That total, complete, all consuming love. Let's see the possibilities within ourselves. For they really are endless. We are all children of God. We were put on this Earth for a reason and it is our job to figure out what that reason is. We are safe and loved unconditionally. We can do and be anything we want to be. So, together let's take these steps and many more, and move ourselves into the land of Endless Possibilities.

Oh the places you'll go,
Today is your day!
Your mountain is waiting,
So . . . get on your way!

~ Dr. Seuss, *Oh, the Places You'll Go!*

Much Love, Laura

Laura McGill is a two-time graduate of the Institute of Children's Literature. She is currently working on a young adult historical novel and is in the process of completing her Bachelor's Degree in Metaphysical Sciences. You can find Laura at her new blog **www.authorlauramcgill.com**

People frequently believe the creative life is grounded in fantasy. The more difficult truth is that creativity is grounded in reality, in the particular, the focused, the well-observed or specifically imagined.

~ Julia Cameron

Bonus Day

Today, I choose a thought of

Creative Expression

by Patricia Hayes

Your life is a unique creative expression of You.

You are the only one who can:

Shine your Light

Speak your Truth

Share your Love

We stand on the edge of our world wondering what will happen next. We feel an intense force moving but aren't sure what our feeling means. Some fear what will happen and others seem to know that human consciousness is expanding and an industrial and spiritual revolution is just beginning to occur.

Many scientists around the world have already demonstrated that all matter exists in a vast quantum web. We are not just a chemical reaction, as once thought, but an energetic charge, and all living things are a coalescence of energy in a field of energy that is connected to every other thing in the world. We connect with each other at the very core of our being. This field of energy is a life force flowing through the universe, which in the past has been typically called the collective consciousness by psychologists and Holy Spirit by theologians. You can best image the collective consciousness as a humongous thought warehouse with many floors that reach into the sky. Bottom floors house the lowest and darkest thoughts within mankind and the highest floors contain the most enlightened ones. Typically the daily thoughts that rise within most people are found midway and that is rapidly changing.

In this time of great transition, we are moving from the basic dinosaur thinking of our self, life, world, universe, and cosmos to the mindset of a superman. Superman moves fast. There is no place he can't go. He has his own propulsion which is thought. He rights wrongs wherever needed. The word *try* is not included in his thoughts. Everything he does, he does with his Knowing. He knows that he can do whatever is needed at each moment. Because of this, he fears nothing. He uses his powers for good and nothing else. He is free to use his super powers for others for he takes care of his own needs.

The new and emerging views are telling us that there is unity and purpose to our world. We no longer stand on the outside looking in. What we do and think is critical in creating our world. What we do and what we think matters to the whole of Mankind. We are all collectively creating our world moment by moment. The Power of One inspired person has the ability to inspire thousands, and through their words, ideas, discoveries, and creative expression they in turn inspire billions. You, through your desire and inspired thought, can lift the collective pool of thought that rises within the minds of mankind each day.

Your work is a unique creative expression of You.
Your work is your instrument for self-expression.

No matter what kind of work we do, from running a household to a private practice or working in industry, our work can become one of our most engaging and fulfilling areas. *The way you see your job is how you respond to your job.* What you see depends on what eyes you look through. If our only reason to have a job is to survive, we resent our work. The fact that we are working for someone other than self could cause judgment, resentment, and hostility. We could feel that our employer is stealing our time when we could be doing something we value and enjoy. If this is our attitude, we are bored at work rather than happy. We have never realized that we are truly working for our *self* and the jobs we have are our opportunities for self-expression. The truth of the matter is that if we put no joy into our work, our work will give us no joy. If you enjoy your work, congratulate yourself and say "well done." When we recognize and accept our work as more than a paycheck or something that has to be done, we are able to be both successful and inspirationally engaged at work.

Work by its very nature is ever-changing, unpredictable, and an opportunity for our Light to shine.

If our attitude about work is ho-hum, we must lift our thoughts, emotions, and vision to see and experience work and our self in a totally new authentic way. We must release attachment to being perfect and appreciate and believe in who we already are because we realize the progress we've made. We understand that we and our work are not separate. *Our work is an extension of our thinking, feeling, and being. Our workplace is an opportunity to reflect our excellence and creative expression.*

Today, I will contemplate expanding my Creative Expression.

Creative Expression is the result of successfully combining several specific ingredients. If we want to broaden our scope and expand our creative expression, we must think holistically. We must acknowledge our whole self—body, mind, and spirit. All are important to our well-being. We must go within and acknowledge our varied basic needs and desires rather than ignoring them as we often do. Knowing what we want allows us to give birth to new creative expression that will fulfill the whole of us. The first ingredient to enhancing and expanding your creative expression is determining and declaring what you want.

Ingredient #1 – Knowing What You Want
Knowing what you want matters greatly!

Today, I will Clarify and Declare what I want in my life.

Clarifying what you want is feeling with and thinking about what you want. Declaring what you want is to know what you want and state it in some way. You must be able to define your physical, emotional-mental, and spiritual aspirations and be able to express them in words before they can manifest in your life. You matter! To know what you want is the first step of being a creator.

Ingredient #2 – Desire

Sometimes our thoughts prod us to do something that is good for us just because we should. However, we really don't feel any desire to do it. Intention without desire cannot take form. Read each statement below slowly, pausing to feel with each one. Place a check beside any that spark a feeling of *desire*. You will feel energy within your body if you identify with and feel desire for any on the list. (Add your own inspirations if these don't resonate with you.)

- ❑ I want harmony in my life and beauty in my environment.
- ❑ I want to detach from dramas and have more time to nourish myself.
- ❑ I want to feel self-worth and self-esteem as I journey through life.
- ❑ I want greater clarity to stay focused and lovingly take charge of situations.
- ❑ I want to love and feel loved and surround myself with loving relationships.
- ❑ I want greater balance in my career and home life.
- ❑ I want peace of mind and a greater sense of abundance in my life.

❑ I want to feel greater clarity, purpose, and direction.

❑ I want to work my creative magic and accomplish the things that are meaningful to me.

❑ I want to release my attachment to being perfect and feel good about my progress.

❑ I want to trust myself and follow my heart and dreams with persistence.

❑ I want to feel and know my goodness, express wisdom every day, and Create, Create, Create.

Place the list where you can see and read it often. At the end of the day, read the list again and choose the three things you most desire in your life. List the three and place these where you can see them often. You can work on some of the others later when you begin to see evidence of progress with the three you chose. When you complete this, you are ready to add the third Ingredient.

Ingredient #3 – Imagination

Knowing what you want gives you the Desire to pursue what you want. Imagination increases your desire and continually births the inspired thoughts necessary to manifest what you want.

Today, I will take time for me and nourish my imagination.

I have found, without a shadow of a doubt, that **knowing what you want, desire, and imagination which births inspired thought** are our inherent creation tools. We need all three and must combine them in that order to create successfully all the time. We live on the edge of darkness the collective ignorance of Mankind. Darkness reveals itself to us every day. We see struggle, poverty, hatred, violence, prejudice, fear, domination, and the list goes on and on.

Each of us that is reading this book or has contributed to this book stands on the edge of darkness. This isn't negative. It's a positive thing to do. We have consciously chosen the edge because we care about bringing greater light into our lives and our world. We know that if anyone trapped in darkness is searching for a greater way, they will be attracted to our light and hopefully inspired by us to find their own light. Light transforms the darkness of ignorance and is the source of our wisdom, love, harmony, beauty, inspiration, courage, compassion, creative expression, and the list could go on and on. We choose the light of wisdom rather than ignorance, solutions rather than problems, harmony rather than chaos, and unity rather than prejudice and hatred. Through our inspirations and creative expression, we act as way showers for others to realize their own courage, solutions, and creative expression.

We have to remind ourselves often not to fall into the darkness. Sometimes, however, we do slip and a barrage of negative thoughts and feelings besiege us along with a bevy of self-judgments. Self-doubt fills us when we are in the darkness because we can't see or feel our light. The weight of our light, however, is always greater and we realize what happened. We imagine ourselves once again standing on the edge. Our imagination inspires the inspirational thoughts necessary to lift ourselves and continue sharing our inspirations and creative expression.

Imagination is the divine tool that takes us on a journey from where we are to where we want to be. Imagination, which Kabbalists call the Diaphane or the Translucent, is really the eye of the soul. It is the mirror of visions of things unseen. Hermes Trismegistus named this magic agent the grand Telesma, because when it produces radiance it is called light. He knew it to be that substance which was created by God before all else when God said, "Let there be light."

Imagination is substance and motion at one and the same time; it is fluid and a perpetual vibration that becomes magnetic light when activated by our will. It is the Great Magic Agent and apparatus of the Magi. The words *spiritual* and *material* merely express degrees in the density of substance. What we call imagination in man is the inherent faculty of the soul to assimilate to itself the images and reflections contained in the living light, or the great magic agent—imagination. Through the magical agent of imagination, man discovers new worlds, cures diseases, modifies the weather, flies to the moon, and resuscitates the heart, because imagination exalts the will and gives it unlimited power. Walt Disney certainly understood and delighted us with this mysterious power for many years.

Our ability to imagine is our ability to image our dreams and visions within our mind's eye. Imagination is a spiritual gift we all have and use. Understanding imagination and knowing its power to beneficially transform our lives is profoundly eye-opening. Now is the time to activate your imagination and expand your creative expression by imaging the three things you most want in your life.

Find a quiet and comfortable place, close your eyes, take a few deep breaths, and relax. Imagine yourself in situations at home and at work, living, enjoying, and benefiting by the new specific things you are now feeling in your life. As you imagine yourself fulfilled and living in this new way, be very observant of your thoughts and feelings. With imagination you can do anything. Tune into and listen to your inspired thoughts and notice how wonderful you feel. When you are through, record any of the inspired thoughts you discovered. *Know that you are on the path that inspires creative expression and will enjoy every step you take.*

Patricia Hayes is an artist and author of five books and has appeared on numerous television programs including *A Current Affair*. She has been a pioneer in intuitive and spiritual development for 45 years and is known for her innovative teaching methods. Patricia is the founder of Delphi University in McCaysville, Georgia. **www.delphiu.com**

If you could only sense how important you are to the lives of those you meet, how important you can be to the people you may never even dream of. There is something of yourself that you leave at every meeting with another person.

~ Fred (Mr.) Rogers

Christian Belz

Christian Belz has been a practicing architect in Metro Detroit for 28 years and is a member of Detroit Working Writers. He won the Grand Prize in Aquarius Press's 2011 Bright Harvest Prize for his short story. His fiction has appeared in Writers' Journal, The Storyteller Magazine, and Wicked East Press's anthology *Short Sips, Coffee House Flash Fiction Collection 2*. His poetry has been published in WestWard Quarterly and Yes, Poetry. He is a three-time semifinalist in the Summer Literary Seminars' annual competition.

Christian is seeking publication of his first murder mystery *The Accused Architect*, which features architect Ken Knoll, whose well-meaning intern moves a dead body from a project site to prevent a delay in the construction schedule. Now the body has disappeared and Ken is driven to find it and solve the crime before repercussions ruin the firm.

In Ken Knoll's second architectural mystery *The Civic Center Corpse*, a millionaire donor to the city's auditorium project is crushed and killed when the sign bearing his name tumbles from the building Ken designed. After he shows that foul play was involved, the dead man's widow implores Ken to find the murderer.

www.ChristianBelz.org

Sandy Weaver Carman

Sandy Weaver Carman partners with writers, speakers, trainers, and coaches, taking work they've already done and turning it into a revenue river.

She is the CEO of Voicework on Demand, Inc., an audio production company specializing in audio books and products. She's a sought-after presenter, teaching people how to use audio production software, as well as working with organizations to get their staff moving in the same direction—towards success!

She's the award-winning author of *The Original MBA – Succeed in Business Using Mom's Best Advice* and uses stories from that book in her corporate and nonprofit seminars.

To book Sandy to speak at your event, email her at **sandy@voiceworkondemand.com**.

To find out how Voicework On Demand, Inc. can help you build your own revenue river, visit **www.voiceworkondemand.com**

To connect with Sandy on Facebook, LinkedIn, Twitter, and Google+, visit **http://about.me/SandyWeaverCarman**

Kristin Colier

Dedicated to a life of learning and personal growth, Kristin Colier finds adventure and inspiration in creative writing, public speaking, and stand-up and improvisational comedy. She is an ordained minister, firewalker and award-winning songwriter.

An innovator at heart, and a user-experience strategist for over 20 years, Kristin finds creative business solutions to allow people to have more positive interactions with technology and help businesses connect with their customers in more meaningful ways.

She holds Bachelor of Science degrees in Mechanical Engineering from The Georgia Institute of Technology and Mathematics from SUNY Oneonta.

After a major career and relationship transition, Kristin had a crash course in spiritual growth and manifestation. She started daily meditation, visualization and affirmations, and inspired by great thought leaders and motivators such as Wayne Dyer, Eckhart Tolle, Deepak Chopra and Tony Robbins she continues to pursue her life purpose: using her optimism, enthusiasm, knowledge, and creativity to support, inspire, and collaborate with others to create innovative solutions for a more harmonious future and to love, learn, grow, and have fun in the process.

She aspires to live a life of example and inspiration spreading messages of compassion, gratitude, love, and forgiveness to help others live happier, more fulfilling lives.

Join Kristin for a cup of abundance and joy at **www.daydreamcafe.com.**

Martha Forlines

Martha Forlines is a successful, nationally recognized leadership consultant, coach, author, speaker, and President of Belief System Institute (BSI). Her expertise is employee motivation and engagement. She has creative solutions for underperforming leaders, teams, or organizations that work!

Martha co-authored a book for women leaders and leaders of women with Thad Green entitled *Inspiring Women . . . BECOMING Courageous, Wise Leaders.* The book speaks to women developing the confidence for extraordinary leadership, understanding the three keys to wisdom, and having the courage to make a difference.

BSI has been improving performance by 70% for employees participating in their programs for over twenty years. Martha likes using a multi-disciplinary approach with her clients, using DISC behavior style tools, Thad Green's theory of motivation and engagement, and appreciative inquiry to connect the dots quickly across organizations to improve results.

678-576-5207
www.beliefsysteminstitute.com

Betty Humphrey Fowler

Betty Humphrey Fowler has a Bachelor of Science degree in Physical Education and was the head fitness instructor for the Police and Fire Academies at the Santa Rosa Jr. College Regional Training Center in Northern California. For 17 years, she taught job-related and lifetime fitness skills to over 3,000 police and fire academy recruits.

Betty had begun studying Feng Shui when her husband, a career police officer and SWAT team sniper, developed an acute case of Post-Traumatic Stress Disorder (PTSD). She used Feng Shui principles to improve the energy in their home to support his healing. Both she and her husband, Wes, believe that the changes had a profound positive impact on how the entire family survived this very stressful situation.

Betty is a Certified Interior Re-designer and Feng Shui Consultant trained in Essential Feng Shui by internationally recognized Feng Shui expert Terah Kathryn Collins, at the Western School of Feng Shui. She has helped many clients going through life-changing events shift the energy in their living spaces to assist in the healing process and renew their enthusiasm for life. Betty offers private consultations (in person and online), workshops, and speaking engagements.

Contact Betty through her blog **www.feelgoodinyourspace.com** or through her business website **www.interiorsandupholstery.com**.

David Greer

Marketing and media entrepreneur David Greer believes it all starts with a story.

For more than 30 years, David has harnessed the creative tools of the day to tell the stories of clients and causes—in print, online, through photography, video, film, and song—to achieve concrete business goals. From his earliest successes in economic development, strategic planning, and publishing to newer endeavors in music and film, his storytelling craft and business acumen have gained a national and international reputation.

An entrepreneur at heart, David launched marketing and media firm Tillman Allen Greer in 1996, recently morphing the firm into Story Road, a content marketing agency for the digital age. His imaginative marketing insight and strategic consulting expertise have proven successful for a diverse mix of clients, particularly in the marketing of technical products and services.

In the consulting realm, David is an idea practitioner for select clients, providing innovative strategic and business development guidance. He is also considered an expert in market-driven strategy for college organizations.

Always searching for excellence and delving deeper to find the best practices to achieve it, David views life through a lens that brings relevance into focus for every opportunity.

www.storyroad.com

Kelly Greer

Kelly Greer is a summa cum laude graduate of the "Been there, ought not to have done that" School of Bad Decisions. Kelly brings a realness, compassion, and a deeply personal understanding of God's amazing grace and help that is available for all who seek it. A gifted encourager and self-described "show me the steps" analytic, Kelly offers step-by-step help to living a life of peace, purpose, love, and happiness regardless of current circumstances or an "exciting" past.

Today, Kelly is the publisher of Gwinnett Magazine and co-owner with her husband, David, of a full-service advertising agency outside of Atlanta, Georgia. Kelly is a graduate of Leadership Gwinnett and is active on many boards in our community including the Gwinnett Chamber of Commerce. She also serves on the Board of Directors at Fusion Church in Buford. Kelly and David live in Buford with their ever-emptying nest, two neurotic dogs, a half dead fish, and a tailless gecko.

www.gwinnettmagazine.com

Andy Greider

Andy "Google Me" Greider is the founder of the Robin Hood Business Growth Model, where he leverages his experience and network to help companies grow at no direct cost to them. The business model is based on the idea that you should only take back what you can give out.

Andy also acts as a business consultant and defacto VP of Marketing for many companies. He is an author of both fiction and nonfiction books, myriad blog posts and articles, and hosts two radio shows (**www.uniquenessispower.biz** and **www.relaxhr.com.**) He has recently been hired as a sales trainer and motivational speaker. Having worked in about every field possible, he is always looking for a new challenge or opportunity to grow.

Andy enjoys helping others, committing random acts of kindness (thanks to the teachings of his parents), and teaching his son to pay everything forward. In his perfect world, you'll find Andy with the ones he loves, in nature, listening to inspiring music, and dancing under the stars.

Learn more at: **www.robinhoodbusinessgrowth.com**

Patricia Hayes

Patricia Hayes is an artist and author of five books. Patricia has been a leading pioneer in intuitive and spiritual development for over 45 years and is well known for her innovative experiential teaching methods. Patricia and her husband, Marshall, founded Delphi University in the beautiful Blue Ridge Mountains of North Georgia in 1985 and presently have graduates from 42 countries. Delphi University is a well-known world-renowned school of higher learning offering numerous Certification Courses, and Bachelors, Masters, and Doctorate level degree programs. The University website is **www.delphiu.com**. Marshall is a retired Vice President of the Kimberly-Clark Corporation.

Patricia also is the founder of The RoHun Institute, which offers an extensive study program in Spiritual Psychotherapy and Transpersonal Psychology. She has also developed a Self-Enlightenment Correspondence Program that is offered on the website **www.selfenlighten.com**.

Patricia is currently working on her new book *Light from the Heavens*, featuring art as a spiritual experience. Her book includes her latest art pieces and commentary on the new art that is emerging in our world today. Contact Patricia at **patriciahayes7@centurylink.net** or view her website at **patriciahayesart.com**.

Jim Hogan

Jim Hogan is a trainer with the Referral Institute who speaks to companies and groups on networking, referral marketing, and leveraging social media to reach their niche market and explode sales. If you are not using LinkedIn® to make the right connections, then you need to talk with Jim.

Jim's passion for life and constant desire to learn has opened new doors to creativity. He co-authored *Improv to Improve Your Business* in 2011 as a collaborative effort during his study of improv comedy with Blank Stage in Marietta, Georgia.

His competitive nature shines through and during his third year competing in shorter distance triathlons, he completed his first IRONMAN® distance Triathlon (swim 2.4 miles , bicycle 112 miles, run 26.2 miles) in November 2012 at IRONMAN® Florida. Jim continues to officiate ice hockey for USA Hockey youth programs and ACHA college level games.

Jim grew up in the Maryland suburbs of Washington, D.C., is happily married to Cathy Hogan, and has been an Atlanta resident since 1993. He holds a BS degree in Business Finance from the University of Delaware, and is a Certified Networker® II Instructor and an active member of the National Speakers Association's Georgia Chapter.

Contact Jim: 404-375-8546

        www.linkedin.com/in/jimhogan

        www.JimHogan.net

Dr. Robin Kirby

Dr. Robin Kirby is a Heart Centered Therapist, combining traditional cognitive techniques with hypnotherapy, regressive therapy, conscious connected breathing, meditation, and guided imagery to find the source of troubling emotions and patterns to facilitate healing at the deepest level for her clients. She provides a nurturing environment that allows individuals, couples, and family members to open their hearts and live from that place of authenticity.

Her passion is working at the soul level with her clients, helping them to connect with their inner spark and the essence and source of their life force energy. Her goal is to see each and every person whom she touches living vibrantly and joyously, touching others to bring more compassion and healing into the world.

Robin holds a Masters Degree in Education and a PhD in Clinical Psychology. She is a Certified Clinical Hypnotherapist, Certified Release Therapist, Certified Life Coach, and Educator. She is also a Reiki practitioner and is constantly studying, learning, and incorporating new energetic and spiritual healing modalities into her work. She is the founder of Loving Impact, a private practice dedicated to the healing of mind, body, and spirit.

www.lovingimpact.com

Ginnie Faye Liman

Ginnie Faye Liman is a published author, copywriter, and fashion journalist. At *Women's Wear Daily*, Ginnie covered five fashion markets. She launched Wordsworth, providing freelance ad copy services to companies including General Foods, IBM, and Cunard Lines Ltd. She designed themes for flyers, ads, and direct mail pieces which appeared in *The New York Times*, *New York Post*, and major magazines. Ferreting out the behind-the-scenes stories of retail marketing, Ginnie wrote *The Re-Designing of A City*, the story of urban renewal of the city of White Plains, NY. The book was an instrumental tool in the acquisition of ten Cadillac-Fairview malls by JMB Realty, resulting in a multi-million dollar real estate deal. Ginnie wrote a manual for The Ford Motor Co., a tool describing how to set up and run a successful Ford Dealership.

Ginnie generated 100 articles for a tri-county Celebrity Fair featuring Willie Nelson, Kenny Rogers, The Monkees, and David Copperfield. As PR Director for Lord & Taylor she circulated press releases, pitched story ideas, and initiated themes for special events. In 1998 she founded Initial Impact Inc., an idea company with a menu of writing and marketing services. Presently, Ginnie is writing a third book devoted to future health care needs, set to be published in the summer of 2013.

Contact Ginnie: **678-777-6729**
404 841-8942
Gliman@bellsouth.net

Nanette Littlestone

Nanette Littlestone works with inspirational authors who struggle to create a clear message and offers specialized guidance to help them write with clarity and passion. She is a writing coach, editor, author, speaker, and food lover. Her passions are chocolate (she owned a gourmet brownie company), art (origami butterflies decorate an entire wall), relationships (the ins and outs of love), and, of course, words. Two of her favorite books are Roget's Thesaurus and the Merriam Webster's unabridged dictionary.

Nanette firmly believes that the world needs more good writing. Nearly 20 years of experience with both fiction and nonfiction kindle her passion for helping authors achieve their own unique message. She regularly works with award-winning authors, has recently co-authored two Easy Weekly Meals electronic cookbooks, and her poetry and short stories have appeared in various online publications and printed anthologies. She also contributes writing articles to numerous blogs and has led a critique group for over 10 years.

Contact Nanette: nanette@wordsofpassion.com
www.wordsofpassion.com
www.nanettelittlestone.com

Traci Long

Traci is an innovative, dynamic, and seasoned professional with a proven talent for building high profile organizations by identifying successful revenue models. She has a client base that includes small- to medium-sized local, national, and international businesses in a variety of media-focused industries.

Traci was formerly the CEO of Ladies Who Launch and is credited with the buildout of a Franchise Media Model for LWL Franchising, LLC.

She has developed successful revenue-generating business models, joint venture collaborations, and partnership opportunities which have consistently enhanced competitive marketing positioning, won favorable media recognition, and supported substantial revenue growth through ThreeDM Communications Inc, a company she founded in 2004.

Traci has a proven track record in launching new businesses and directing operations for successful businesses throughout North America. She is integral in the brand conception and start-up implementation of revenue strategies for businesses that continue to grow financially in the marketplace. She currently develops marketing strategy for Microsoft's Small Business Server Division. Traci facilitates workshops and classes in cities across the country including Stanford University, has been featured on CNN, and is a member of the National Speakers Association.

www.facebook.com/tracilong
@tracilong
www.tracilong.com

Vanessa Lowry

Vanessa Lowry is an author, entrepreneur, radio host, speaker, graphic designer, and marketing consultant. She leverages thirty years of design and marketing expertise to support book authors who are self-publishing.

Her books include: *30 Days of Gratitude; Improv to Improve Your Business; Publishing as a Marketing Strategy;* and *The 28-Day Thought Diet.* Vanessa envisioned the concepts, selected collaborators, co-authored, designed, and formatted the books. She also co-authored *Write a Book – Change the World* with Dr. Tim Morrison.

Vanessa hosts *Art as Worship,* a weekly radio show on Empower Radio. On the show, she interviews artists of various faiths, working in a wide range of media, on the common theme of how they use inspiration and creativity as an expression of their spirituality. Vanessa is also the regular guest host of the radio show *Write Here, Write Now* on Business RadioX.

She is often a featured speaker at events and conferences. A partial listing includes the North Fulton Chamber of Commerce, Kennesaw State University, Georgia Writers Association, Atlanta Theosophical Society, Georgia Center for Non-Profits, Rotary, Kiwanis, American Business Women's Association (ABWA), Johnson Ferry Baptist Women's Retreat, and Robert H. Schuller Institute for Successful Church Leadership.

Contact Vanessa: **www.connect4leverage.com**
www.artasworship.net
www.writeherewritenow.businessradiox.com

Cheryl Anne McGill

Cheryl Anne McGill, RN, MBA, DD, MscD, is a life-partner, mother, grandmother, internationally renowned psychic medium, medical intuitive, radio host, motivational speaker, interfaith minister, and author. Born a spiritual medium, Cheryl Anne has over 50 years of experience conveying messages of love from those in other dimensions and educating thousands about death and dying, quantum physics, and spirituality.

Tested as a "Legitimate and Genuine Psychic Medium," Cheryl Anne appears on Best Psychic Mediums as "The Psychic Medium Who Got Ten Times More Positive Reviews Than Over 400 Psychics & Mediums."

As an advocate of human rights, and a visible lesbian, she works toward raising the vibration of the planet by creating a loving experience of co-existence with everyone as Divine Mind. Cheryl Anne believes that when everyone is in alignment with Divine Mind they are in a state to Love ALLways®—always and in all ways.

Cheryl Anne is blessed to share her life with her life partner and twin soul, Jeanie Ward, and their two dogs, Sugar and Zoey. For more information, visit her website at **www.PsychicEnterprises.com**.

Join Cheryl Anne on Twitter at **@PsychicCheryl** and on Facebook at **www.Facebook.com/PsychicMediumCherylAnne**.

Laura McGill

Laura McGill is a full-time mom, part-time Administrative Assistant, and lifetime student. Residing in Ontario, Canada with her husband and two-year-old son, she spends her days juggling many passions, including writing. Holding two diplomas in Writing for Children and Teenagers, Laura hopes to bring a fresh new voice to the world of writing, with a special interest in the young adult market. As the daughter of psychic medium Cheryl Anne McGill, intuition and Spirit communication run strong in her blood. "I hope to enhance children's faith and connection to spirit through my writing, while touching on real issues that affect their daily lives. And always, always give them a happy ending!"

You can find Laura at her new blog **www.authorlauramcgill.com**

Tricia Molloy

Tricia Molloy is a motivational speaker on change management and leadership through wise business practices.

Organizations like Kimberly-Clark, WellStar Health System, and the Project Management Institute hire Tricia to inspire their people to perform at their best every day. She is the author of *Working with Wisdom: 10 Universal Principles for Enlightened Entrepreneurs* and the *CRAVE Your Goals! and DESIGN Your Ideal Life* e-books.

Known as "The Queen of Serene," Tricia's wise, peaceful presence and common-sense advice are welcome in today's challenging, complex business environment. Through Working with Wisdom talks, workshops, webinars, and retreat programs, Tricia inspires people to achieve their goals faster and easier by capitalizing on life-changing principles—like visualization, affirmations, and gratitude—and the power of the subconscious mind.

For women entrepreneurs and professionals who want to enjoy more success at work and in life, Tricia also offers one-on-one, three-month Wisdom Mentoring.

On a personal note, Tricia and her husband, Rick, live in the Atlanta suburb of Marietta with their teenage twins, Connor and Allyson, and their joyful Golden Retrievers, Honey and Lucy. They spend part of the year playing at their beach home in Gulf Shores, Alabama.

www.triciamolloy.com

Jennifer Moore

Jennifer Moore is a Licensed Clinical Social Worker and the owner of ISIS Consulting, LLC. Her mission is to Inspire Solution in Service which she does through counseling, coaching, consulting, and trainings. She is currently working on two books and a workbook that will launch in 2013. In addition to direct practice with clients, Jennifer is very engaged in community organiza-  tions and development. She is also a motivational speaker for both large and small organizations.

Jennifer is a marathon-runner and self-proclaimed yogi, the mother of one son and two bonus daughters, two four-legged boys, Leo and Griffin, and is happily married to her best friend.

www.isisconsultingllc.com

Monserrat del Carmen Pineda

Monserrat was anointed into a world of mysticism at an early age. Born in Chile, her extra sensory talents and enlightenment were influenced by a lifetime of mystical and unexplained phenomena. Encounters with Angelic Beings and Emissaries of Light, along with benevolent UFOs, encoded Monserrat with higher frequency vibrations. Monserrat weaves light within her energy field, profoundly accelerating consciousness for those on the ascension path.

After receiving a Bachelor's Degree in Communications from the University of Iowa, Monserrat worked in the corporate arena nearly 20 years. Taking a purposeful hiatus to raise her children, she soon discovered enhanced abilities after apprehensively participating in a contest sponsored by the Coast to Coast AM radio show with Art Bell. A show with millions of listeners worldwide, Monserrat accurately described the target placed within a sealed envelope. She was invited to further enhance her Technical Remote Viewing abilities directly with Major Ed Dames, a high-ranking VIP involved in the Stargate program.

Both traditionally schooled and "spirit trained," she travels and studies with masters, healers, shamans, and mystics. Monserrat was initiated into a 1,000-year-old long lineage of Mayan healers and Ordained in 2003. She lives in north Georgia with her husband and two children, where she consults and works on her book.

monserratdelcarmen@comcast.net
www.monserratdelcarmen.com

Kathryn Sener

Kathryn (Kathy) Sener is a producer, writer, mentor, and communicator who utilizes a creative approach for enterprises to tell their stories with simplicity and, most importantly, become an educational experience  worth repeating. Kathy's past success in sales, relationship management and new market entry is attributed to working closely with clients on accurate problem identification, diagnosis and providing recommendations, tools, and resources necessary to achieve the maximum increase in the shortest amount of time. Her ability to create, adapt, educate, and inspire action and understanding is based on using a themed approach to reach the audience. Her style propels sales and management performances in competitive environments.

Watching sales teams deliver uninformative, long, and uneventful presentations, Kathy identified a niche to critique and enhance the product showcasing opportunities. Her partnering skills bring the right parties together to build and deliver successful growth. Kathy's work today includes the ensemble aspects of theater to approach viewers.

Kathy's love for the arts has transformed her style and business acumen to bringing the art of a consistent theme to create success in a message or event treating each opportunity to learn as a Sought-After Event.

ZEALOUS   VISIONARY   CONCEPTUAL   PIONEERING

Contact Info: **www.knewstage.com**
770-733-1800

Sharon S. Smith

Sharon S. Smith, retired with 20 years in technology management and sales and 5 years in healthcare, divides her passions for wellness through her company Thrive Nutrition and the development of its brand and product line along with community advocacy.

Her latest endeavor in North Metro Atlanta is to raise funds for first responders to equip them with pet lifesaving gear through her Oxygen Fur Pets project.

She delights in creating a thriving home filled with her love for food and cooking, organic gardening, decorating, close friends, and caring for her animal companions. She shares her thriving home with an incredible husband; her precious Shih Tzu, Zoe; and Oscar, Kato, and Izzy—the cat trio whose job is to construct and enforce most of the rules of their home.

www.thrivenutrition.net
www.facebook.com/OxygenFurPets

Mindy Strich

Mindy Strich is a certified IEM Energetic Healing Facilitator, Reiki Practitioner, and Ordained Minister. A successful business woman, Mindy endured a lifelong battle with an unknown chronic illness. After 25 years of seeking traditional medical solutions, she enrolled in a two-year course at The White-winds Institute to find a solution to the health issues that had plagued her most of her life. Studying with Dr. Fernand Poulin, one of the leading voices in energy medicine, Mindy's training enabled her to explain her illness, transform her health, and heal from the unexpected end of her marriage. Owner of Healing Hearts, LLC, she is now assisting clients on their own path to healing.

Mindy facilitates a monthly women's "Heartache to Healing" support group directed at women who are facing separation and divorce. She is also the co-promoter of "The Good Karma Group," a social networking group for spiritually inspired women in the Atlanta area.

www.healingheartenergy.com
www.facebook.com/#!/healingheartsllc
www.meetup.com/Womens-Healing-from-Seperation-Loss-and-Divorce
Twitter: @MindyStrich

Jeanie Ward

Jeanie Ward is a gifted speaker, author, mentor, interfaith minister, meditation facilitator, women's whole life coach, and energy medicine practitioner.

A modern day mystic, Jeanie's vision vitalizes people to see beyond the illusion of separation, awakening them to the Oneness of Life. For over 30 years, she has inspired and challenged people to step outside of their comfort zone, to live authentically and to love unconditionally.

Many lifetime challenges, including emotional eating, obesity, zero self-esteem, depression, ADD, and a breast cancer journey in 2002 offered Jeanie transformational opportunities for her soul's emergence and expansion.

Whether speaking to audiences, presenting seminars, or working one on one with a client, Jeanie's desire and commitment is to shine her heart-light brilliantly, so that others may discover their inner and outer beauty and divinity.

Jeanie serves on the ministerial team at Unity North Atlanta in Georgia. She is blessed with a beautiful life partner and twin soul, Cheryl Anne McGill, and two divine "dogters," Sugar and Zoey.

Jeanie is affectionately known as "The Dog Jeanie," because of her magical, "paw"erful, mind-body-heart-soul work with canines and their human companions.

www.jeanieward.com
www.facebook.com/jeanie.ward.3
(USA) 770-317-1954

Kyle Young

Throughout her career, Kyle Young has led teams in creating dynamic, diverse, and award-winning solutions—from generating effective ideas, to designing branding programs, ad campaigns, and interactive displays. Founding what became one of Atlanta's Top 50 Advertising Agencies, her vision has been recognized with over 75 highly competitive awards.

Today, Kyle continues to inspire and teach through her speaking and writing, to consult and create on-target ideas for her clients, and to mentor a select group of entrepreneurs. Called the "Project Whisperer" by some, and "business big sister" by a few, all know that Kyle's focus is on helping them succeed. They trust her experience and count on her for deep conversation and probing questions. Her concentrated listening peels back the layers to get to the core, and her solutions are based on their needs, budgets, and situations.

Authentic feedback. Legitimate advice. Ideas based on real life experiences and wide-open creativity. Kyle brings her extensive network of trusted resources, award-winning designers, valued partners, and key connections to every relationship. Trust Kyle to mix all the key ingredients, knowing that the end result will be flawless.

You can find Kyle blogging at **www.Multi-TaskingWoman.com** and sharing her secrets for for business and life at **www.EffectiveIdeas.com**.

Contact Kyle: **www.EffectiveIdeas.com**
770-818-0022
Facebook: **Multi-TaskingWoman**
Twitter: **@multitasking**

Index of Authors

Thank you for joining us in
The 28-Day Thought Diet.

Connect with any of the authors
using the contact information
listed on their bios.